BUILT TO LAST A LIFETIME

By

Fidelis Gomes

TABLE OF CONTENT

ACKNOWLEDGEMENT

This book is dedicated with love to my daughter, Josephine, whose unwavering belief in me has been my guiding light. To my beloved wife, Catherine, your endless support and patience have been my greatest strength—I couldn't have done this without you. To my dear parents, now watching over me from heaven, your love and teachings continue to inspire me every day. A heartfelt thanks to Lucas Dawson from Writers Publishing Lab, whose guidance and expertise have been instrumental in bringing this book to life.

My journey as an author has been deeply shaped by the wisdom and inspiration I have gathered from countless books and authors, whose thoughtful words have motivated me. I would like to take this opportunity to express my profound gratitude to each of them—thank you!

This journey would not have been possible without each of you. Thank you from my heart.

INTRODUCTION

Success is often seen as a fleeting achievement—something to be won, celebrated, and then replaced by the next big goal. But true success, the kind that lasts for a lifetime and beyond, is not about quick wins or temporary gains. It is built on a foundation of strong values, meaningful relationships, and a commitment to principles that stand the test of time.

If you want to create a life or an organization that endures, you must look beyond strategies and business tactics. You must first understand the most powerful force behind lasting success—people. A thriving company, a fulfilling career, and a purposeful life all stem from the same source: the character, mindset, and values of the individuals who shape them. Trust, integrity, empathy, and humility are not just admirable qualities; they are the building blocks of something greater—an enduring legacy.

This book is your guide to achieving long-term success, both personally and professionally. It will challenge you to rethink what it means to be successful and encourage you to embrace a mindset that prioritizes simplicity, happiness, and holistic well-being. You will learn how family harmony fuels professional achievements, how maintaining a positive and healthy lifestyle enhances productivity, and why faith in something greater than yourself provides the ultimate source of strength.

Through these principles, you will discover that success is not about working harder or chasing external validation—it is about building something meaningful, something that lasts. Whether you are leading a company, growing a career, or simply seeking to improve your own life, the key to lasting success lies in the choices you make today. By committing to values that withstand time and challenges, you can create a future filled with purpose, fulfillment, and enduring prosperity.

Let's begin this journey together—toward a success that is not just achieved, but sustained for a lifetime.

CHAPTER 1

THE CORE OF EVERY GREAT ORGANIZATION PEOPLE WITH STRONG VALUES

Success in business and life is not determined solely by strategy, technology, or market conditions—it is built on people. At the heart of every thriving organization are individuals who embody strong values, shaping the culture, direction, and sustainability of the business. If you want to build something that lasts, you must start with the right people—people who live by principles such as moral character, trust, respect, and empathy. These qualities are the foundation upon which great companies and institutions stand.

THE POWER OF STRONG VALUES IN AN ORGANIZATION

Think of the most successful and enduring organizations in history. What do they all have in common? Beyond their products, services, or business models, they share one fundamental trait: a strong, values-driven culture. These organizations prioritize honesty, accountability, and integrity, creating workplaces that inspire loyalty, dedication, and long-term success. Their values shape every aspect of their operations, from leadership decisions to daily employee interactions, and this consistency becomes a defining factor in their resilience and growth.

When you surround yourself with people who uphold strong values, you build an organization that is more than just a collection of employees—it becomes a community. A business filled with people who trust one another, respect differing perspectives, and work

4

collaboratively will always outperform one where distrust, dishonesty, and internal competition are the norm. Employees who align with the company's core values bring more than just skills to the table; they contribute to a positive work environment where mutual support and shared goals drive performance.

Strong values serve as the foundation for decision-making. In times of uncertainty or crisis, organizations with a clear set of ethical guidelines are better equipped to navigate challenges without compromising their integrity. Whether it's handling financial difficulties, public relations crises, or leadership transitions, companies with strong values remain steadfast in their commitment to ethical business practices. This stability fosters confidence among employees, customers, and stakeholders, ensuring the organization maintains its reputation and continues to thrive even in turbulent times.

Additionally, a values-driven culture enhances employee engagement and retention. People want to work for organizations that stand for something meaningful. When employees feel connected to a company's mission and values, they are more likely to be passionate about their work and stay with the organization long-term. This reduces turnover, increases productivity, and strengthens overall morale. Employees who believe in the company's purpose go beyond merely fulfilling job responsibilities—they become brand ambassadors, advocating for the organization both inside and outside the workplace.

WHY CHARACTER MATTERS MORE THAN SKILL

Skills can be taught, but character is ingrained. When building a successful organization, it's easy to focus on credentials, experience, and technical abilities. While these are important, they should never take precedence over character. A person's moral compass, work ethic, and emotional intelligence determine how they apply their skills, interact with others, and contribute to a positive work culture. Without these traits, even the most talented employees can be detrimental to an organization's long-term success.

You have likely encountered individuals who are technically brilliant but lack integrity, teamwork, or accountability. At first glance, they may seem like valuable assets, producing impressive results and showcasing expertise. However, over time, their negative traits—whether dishonesty, arrogance, or an unwillingness to collaborate—can erode trust, damage team morale, and create a toxic work environment. A business driven by a culture of negativity or unethical behavior will eventually struggle with high turnover, low productivity, and a damaged reputation.

Instead, organizations should prioritize hiring individuals who demonstrate honesty, accountability, respect, and emotional intelligence. These qualities create an environment where employees are not only skilled but also aligned with the company's values and mission. Employees with strong character take responsibility for their actions, support their colleagues, and contribute to a culture of trust. They lead by example, inspire others, and make decisions that benefit the organization as a whole rather than focusing solely on personal gain.

Leaders who recognize the importance of character in hiring and team development set their organizations up for long-term success. A workplace built on integrity fosters open communication, mutual respect, and a sense of shared purpose. Employees feel valued and motivated, leading to higher engagement, increased productivity, and a commitment to the company's vision.

Moreover, when character and competence go hand in hand, an organization thrives. It becomes a place where employees support one another, conflicts are resolved constructively, and ethical decision-making is the norm. This kind of culture not only benefits the internal workings of a company but also strengthens relationships with clients, partners, and stakeholders. Trust is one of the most valuable assets in business, and trust is built on character.

By making character a priority in hiring and leadership, organizations ensure that their workforce is not only skilled but also principled, dedicated, and aligned with their core values. In the end, skills may help a company grow, but strong character ensures that growth is sustainable and meaningful.

THE ROLE OF TRUST IN BUILDING A RESILIENT TEAM

Trust is the glue that holds an organization together. Without it, no amount of leadership, incentives, or motivational speeches can create a truly unified team. A culture of trust starts from the top—leaders must be transparent, fair, and consistent in their actions. Employees must feel secure in knowing that their contributions are valued and that their leaders have their best interests at heart.

As a leader, you set the tone. Do you encourage open communication? Do your employees feel safe expressing ideas and concerns? When mistakes happen, do you foster a culture of learning rather than blame? Trust is cultivated through everyday interactions, and once established, it creates an environment where individuals are motivated to contribute their best work without fear.

RESPECT AND EMPATHY: THE FOUNDATIONS OF STRONG WORKPLACE RELATIONSHIPS

A thriving organization is one where respect and empathy are non-negotiable values. Respect means recognizing the contributions of every individual, regardless of title or position. It means valuing diverse perspectives and treating everyone with dignity. When people feel respected, they are more engaged, more innovative, and more committed to the success of the organization.

Empathy, on the other hand, is the ability to understand and share the feelings of others. It allows leaders to connect with their teams on a deeper level, to recognize challenges employees face, and to provide support when needed. An empathetic workplace fosters collaboration, reduces conflict, and strengthens bonds between colleagues. Leaders who practice empathy earn the trust and respect of their teams, leading to greater overall morale and productivity.

CREATING A CULTURE THAT FOSTERS INTEGRITY AND ACCOUNTABILITY

Integrity is the foundation of credibility. It ensures that actions align with words, that promises are kept, and that ethical decisions take precedence over short-term gains. When you build an organization rooted in integrity, you attract employees, clients, and partners who share those same values, leading to long-term sustainability.

Accountability goes hand in hand with integrity. A strong organization is one where every individual, from leadership to entry-level employees, takes responsibility for their actions and commitments. When accountability is embedded in the culture, mistakes are acknowledged and corrected rather than hidden or ignored. This openness leads to continuous improvement and strengthens the overall resilience of the organization.

BUILDING A COMPANY CULTURE THAT WITHSTANDS CHALLENGES

Every organization will face difficulties—economic downturns, market shifts, internal crises. However, those built on strong values will have the resilience to withstand and adapt to these challenges. A company culture rooted in trust, respect, and integrity provides the stability needed to navigate turbulent times. While external factors may be unpredictable, an organization's internal strength comes from the values it upholds and the commitment of its people to a shared purpose.

One of the defining traits of a strong company culture is its ability to maintain stability in the face of adversity. When uncertainty arises, organizations with a well-defined culture have a clear foundation to rely on. Employees know what is expected of them, leaders remain consistent in their decision-making, and the company can continue operating with minimal disruption. Without a strong culture, businesses often struggle to maintain cohesion, leading to confusion, misalignment, and disengagement among employees.

During difficult periods, employees look to leadership for guidance. If leaders uphold the organization's core values, they set an example that inspires confidence and unity. Strong leaders recognize that times of crisis are when values matter the most. Instead of reacting with fear or short-sighted decisions, they reinforce the organization's mission, prioritize transparency, and communicate openly with employees. When teams trust their leaders and one another, they can work together to find solutions rather than succumbing to panic or uncertainty. This sense of collective resilience strengthens the company's ability to recover and grow beyond its challenges.

Additionally, a values-driven culture fosters adaptability. Change is inevitable, whether due to industry disruptions, new technologies, or shifts in consumer behavior. Companies with strong cultures are better equipped to evolve because their employees feel secure in their environment. When trust and respect are prioritized, employees are more willing to embrace change, offer innovative solutions, and take calculated risks. This adaptability allows organizations to stay ahead of competitors who struggle with resistance to change or internal conflict.

A strong company culture also plays a crucial role in employee retention and engagement during difficult times. When employees feel valued and supported, they are more likely to remain loyal to the organization, even when external conditions are uncertain. A company that consistently upholds its values—by treating employees fairly, maintaining ethical business practices, and demonstrating a commitment to its mission—earns the trust and dedication of its workforce. In contrast, businesses that abandon their core principles in tough times risk losing their most talented employees, leading to long-term instability.

Moreover, organizations with resilient cultures extend their strength beyond the workplace. Customers, clients, and stakeholders recognize when a company stands by its values, and this trust translates into stronger relationships and brand loyalty. Companies that remain ethical and transparent during crises build reputations that endure beyond temporary hardships. Consumers are more likely to support businesses that demonstrate integrity, and employees take pride in being part of an organization that stands for something greater than just profit.

HOW TO CULTIVATE AND MAINTAIN STRONG VALUES IN YOUR ORGANIZATION

Creating a values-driven culture does not happen by accident—it requires intentional effort. Here are key steps you can take to build and maintain strong values in your organization:

1. Define Your Core Values Clearly

Before you can build a strong organizational culture, you must establish what your company stands for. Core values serve as the foundation for decision-making, behavior, and long-term success. These values should not just be words on a wall or in a mission statement—they must be deeply embedded in your company's daily operations.

Clearly define and communicate your values at every level of the organization. From onboarding new employees to performance evaluations, your values should be a guiding force. Employees should understand what these principles mean in practice and how they translate into daily interactions with colleagues, customers, and stakeholders. When values are consistently reinforced, they become a natural part of the company's identity, guiding actions and fostering a strong, unified culture.

2. Hire and Promote Based on Values

Skills can be trained, but values must align from the start. When hiring, prioritize individuals who demonstrate integrity, intelligence, and energy—but above all, integrity. As Warren Buffett famously said, "If you don't have integrity, intelligence and energy will kill you." A talented and energetic employee without integrity can do more harm than good, undermining trust and stability within your organization. Make integrity a non-negotiable standard in your hiring process, ensuring that every team member contributes to a strong, values-driven culture.

During interviews, ask questions that reveal a candidate's ethical compass, decision-making process, and ability to work collaboratively. Observe how they interact with others and evaluate whether their values align with the organization's mission. The same principles should apply when considering promotions—reward those who exemplify integrity and leadership, not just those with technical expertise. When values drive hiring and promotion decisions, organizations build a foundation of trust, accountability, and long-term success.

3. Setting the Standard Through Actions

As a leader, your behavior shapes the culture of your organization. Employees look to you for guidance, not just in words but in actions. If you want integrity, respect, and accountability to be core values in your workplace, you must consistently demonstrate them yourself.

Leadership is not about demanding compliance; it is about inspiring others through your own conduct. If transparency is a priority, be open and honest in your decision-making. If teamwork is essential, actively collaborate rather than issuing directives from above. When challenges arise, remain ethical and principled in your response, showing that values are non-negotiable, even in difficult situations.

When leaders consistently align their actions with their words, they build trust and create a culture where employees feel motivated to uphold the same standards.

4. Create an Environment of Open Communication

Trust and mutual respect are built through open communication. Employees should feel comfortable voicing concerns, asking questions, and sharing feedback without fear of retaliation. When communication is stifled, misunderstandings arise, morale declines, and employees become disengaged.

Encourage transparency at all levels by creating open-door policies, regular check-ins, and platforms for honest discussion. Foster a culture where employees are not only heard but also valued for their input. When leaders actively listen and respond constructively, they reinforce an environment of trust, collaboration, and continuous improvement.

5. Recognize and Reward Ethical Behavior

If values are truly important to your organization, they should be acknowledged and rewarded. Recognizing employees who consistently demonstrate integrity, teamwork, and accountability reinforces the importance of these principles and encourages others to follow suit.

This recognition does not always have to be monetary. Public praise, leadership opportunities, and career growth can serve as powerful motivators. Employees who see that ethical behavior leads to professional success will be more inclined to uphold the organization's values. By celebrating those who embody the company's principles, you create a culture where doing the right thing is not just expected but genuinely appreciated.

6. Provide Ongoing Training and Development

A values-driven culture is not something that happens once—it requires continuous reinforcement. Offer regular training programs focused on leadership, teamwork, and ethical decision-making to keep employees engaged and aligned with the organization's principles.

Workshops, mentorship programs, and real-world case studies can help employees develop a deeper understanding of how values play out in professional settings. Training should not be limited to new hires; even experienced employees and leaders benefit from periodic refreshers on company ethics, conflict resolution, and workplace culture. Organizations that invest in ongoing development foster a workforce that not only understands the company's values but actively upholds them in every aspect of their work.

7. Hold Everyone Accountable

Accountability is the backbone of a strong organizational culture. Without it, even the most well-defined values become meaningless.

Everyone—from entry-level employees to top executives—must be held to the same ethical standards.

Set clear expectations and enforce them consistently. If an employee or leader violates the organization's values, address the issue promptly and fairly. Accountability does not mean punishment; it means ensuring that actions align with the company's principles. When employees see that integrity is non-negotiable and that everyone is treated equally under the same ethical standards, they are more likely to uphold those values themselves.

Holding people accountable also means giving them the tools to succeed. Provide feedback, coaching, and support to help employees grow. A culture of accountability does not just prevent misconduct—it strengthens trust, reinforces company values, and empowers individuals to take ownership of their actions.

THE LASTING IMPACT OF STRONG VALUES

Organizations that prioritize strong values are not only more successful—they create lasting legacies. When you build a company based on trust, integrity, and respect, you cultivate an environment where people thrive, challenges are met with resilience, and growth is sustainable. The impact of strong values extends far beyond financial success; it creates a workplace where employees feel fulfilled, customers remain loyal, and the organization continues to make a meaningful difference in the world.

As you move forward, ask yourself: Are you building an organization that will last? Are you surrounding yourself with individuals who uphold the values needed for long-term success? The choices you make today will shape the future of your business and life. Choose wisely, invest in character, and watch as your organization stands the test of time.

Building a Life of Purpose: Stories of Integrity and Joy

"Integrity is doing the right thing, even when no one is watching."

- C.S. Lewis

1. The Honest Shopkeeper – Upholding Values in Every Transaction

Mr. Patel ran a small grocery store in his town. Unlike big supermarkets, he knew his customers by name and believed in honesty above all else. One day, a supplier offered him a deal—cheap products that looked the same but were of lower quality. The profit margin was tempting, but Mr. Patel refused.

Months later, a new chain store opened nearby, threatening his business. However, his customers remained loyal. They trusted him because he had never compromised on his values. Over time, his store thrived, proving that integrity in every transaction builds success that no discount can match.

2. The Passionate Teacher – Finding Joy in Work

Emily always dreamed of being a teacher. While her friends chased high-paying corporate jobs, she chose a modest school, where she worked tirelessly to inspire her students. Every lesson was an adventure, every challenge an opportunity.

Years passed, and while others spoke of stress and burnout, Emily felt energized. Teaching wasn't just a job—it was her purpose. The joy she found in her work kept her young at heart, and at 80, she still taught part-time, proving that loving what you do leads to a long and fulfilling life.

3. The Ethical CEO – Integrity in Every Interaction

Jason was the CEO of a growing tech company. Investors pressured him to cut corners to increase profits, but he refused to exploit workers or deceive customers. His leadership was based on fairness, and he treated every employee with respect.

At first, competitors mocked his approach, saying ethics had no place in business. But as scandals toppled other companies, Jason's firm flourished. Employees were loyal, customers trusted them, and his company became an industry leader. He proved that upholding values in every interaction leads not only to success but also to a deeply satisfying life.

CHAPTER 2

THE LINK BETWEEN FAMILY HAPPINESS AND BUSINESS SUCCESS

Success is often viewed as a product of hard work, strategy, and perseverance. While these elements are undoubtedly important, there is another crucial yet frequently overlooked factor—your personal life, particularly the happiness and stability of your family. The connection between a fulfilling home life and success in the workplace is not just theoretical; it has been proven time and time again that when individuals experience joy, support, and emotional well-being at home, they are more likely to thrive professionally.

A happy family life serves as a strong foundation, providing you with the stability, confidence, and motivation needed to excel in your career or business. When your personal life is in harmony, you bring a different level of energy, focus, and resilience to your work. On the other hand, constant stress, conflict, or dissatisfaction at home can create emotional distractions that hinder your ability to perform at your best.

HOW FAMILY HAPPINESS INFLUENCES PROFESSIONAL PERFORMANCE

Your professional success is not just determined by your skills, strategies, or work ethic—it is deeply influenced by the stability and happiness of your personal life. A fulfilling home environment provides emotional support, motivation, and balance, all of which contribute to your effectiveness at work. When your personal relationships are strong, you experience less stress, more focus, and greater resilience, allowing you to navigate professional challenges with confidence and clarity.

Conversely, when your personal life is filled with tension, unresolved conflicts, or emotional distress, your ability to perform at your best is compromised. Workplace productivity suffers when your mind is preoccupied with personal struggles, and decision-making becomes reactive rather than strategic. Below are key ways in which family happiness directly impacts professional performance.

1. Emotional Stability Leads to Better Decision-Making

In business, your ability to make well-informed decisions can determine the success or failure of an endeavor. However, when you are dealing with stress and instability at home, your mind is often preoccupied with personal worries. This distraction can cloud your judgment, making you more impulsive, defensive, or hesitant in your decision-making.

On the other hand, a stable and supportive home environment provides emotional security. When you feel valued and at peace in your personal life, you are more likely to make sound, thoughtful decisions at work. Emotional stability allows you to step back, assess situations objectively, and weigh your options with a long-term perspective. Leaders who experience harmony at home tend to be more composed, confident, and able to handle high-pressure situations effectively.

A calm and secure personal life also fosters patience and emotional intelligence—two critical qualities for effective leadership and collaboration. Whether you are managing a team, negotiating a deal, or addressing a workplace challenge, the ability to remain level-headed and considerate will set you apart.

2. Greater Productivity and Focus

A fulfilling personal life enables you to give your full attention to your work without being weighed down by distractions. When you have unresolved conflicts at home, your thoughts may drift to personal issues even when you are at your desk, attending meetings, or working on important projects. This divided attention can lead to mistakes, inefficiency, and missed opportunities.

Studies show that individuals who experience happiness and stability in their personal lives tend to be more engaged, motivated, and productive at work. They approach tasks with enthusiasm and have a greater ability to maintain concentration. Their work output improves not just in quantity but also in quality.

Moreover, when you feel supported and valued at home, you are less likely to suffer from burnout. Work can be demanding, but a loving and peaceful home environment acts as a restorative space where you can recharge. This balance prevents fatigue and enhances your ability to perform consistently at a high level.

3. Creativity and Innovation Flourish in a Positive Mindset

Innovation is the driving force behind business growth and success, but creativity cannot thrive in an environment of stress and emotional turmoil. When you are constantly worried about personal problems, your brain is in survival mode, focusing on immediate concerns rather than generating fresh ideas.

However, when you feel loved, secure, and emotionally fulfilled at home, your mind is free to explore new possibilities and take calculated risks. Happiness fosters optimism, which in turn encourages creative thinking. You are more likely to embrace challenges as opportunities rather than obstacles.

Happy individuals also tend to be more open-minded and adaptable—two qualities that are essential for innovation. They are willing to experiment, consider different perspectives, and approach problems from unique angles. Companies that encourage employees to maintain a healthy work-life balance often see greater levels of innovation because their teams are mentally refreshed, motivated, and engaged.

4. Resilience in the Face of Adversity

Every professional journey comes with challenges, setbacks, and moments of uncertainty. The difference between those who overcome obstacles and those who struggle often comes down to resilience.

Resilience is not just an internal trait—it is heavily influenced by the support system you have outside of work. When you have a strong, loving family, you have a foundation to fall back on during difficult times. A spouse, children, parents, or close friends who offer emotional support can provide encouragement, perspective, and reassurance when you are facing challenges at work.

This support can make the difference between feeling defeated and finding the strength to push forward. Knowing that you have people who believe in you and stand by your side allows you to navigate setbacks with confidence. Rather than letting failure define you, you see it as a temporary hurdle—one that you have the strength to overcome.

Additionally, family happiness fosters a mindset of long-term thinking. Instead of reacting impulsively to professional difficulties, you are more likely to approach them with patience and perseverance. This resilience not only benefits you personally but also strengthens your leadership abilities, as teams look to leaders who remain composed and solutions-oriented in the face of adversity.

5. Stronger Professional Relationships and Leadership Skills

Your ability to work effectively with colleagues, clients, and employees is directly influenced by your emotional well-being.

People who experience happiness in their personal lives tend to have higher emotional intelligence, which enhances their interpersonal skills.

A stable home life teaches important lessons about communication, empathy, and conflict resolution—skills that are equally valuable in the workplace. If you are accustomed to practicing patience, listening actively, and resolving conflicts in a respectful manner at home, you will naturally apply these skills in professional interactions.

Leaders who prioritize their families often develop a leadership style that is people-focused rather than purely results-driven. They understand the importance of work-life balance, employee well-being, and fostering a positive workplace culture. Employees respect and appreciate leaders who recognize that professional success should not come at the expense of personal fulfillment.

6. The Power of Purpose and Motivation

One of the greatest motivators for success is a sense of purpose. For many people, family provides that purpose. The desire to provide a good life for loved ones, set an example for children, or create a legacy of integrity and success can be powerful driving forces.

When your professional goals are aligned with your personal values and responsibilities, you are more likely to stay committed, work harder, and make choices that lead to long-term success. Instead of chasing short-term gains, you focus on building something meaningful and lasting.

Moreover, family happiness brings a sense of fulfillment that prevents the common pitfall of equating success solely with career achievements. Many professionals climb the corporate ladder only to realize that without strong personal relationships, their accomplishments feel empty. True success is about balance—

achieving professional excellence while nurturing meaningful relationships.

THE ROLE OF WORK-LIFE BALANCE

Achieving harmony between your work and personal life is not just about managing time; it's about setting priorities that align with your values. Many ambitious professionals make the mistake of sacrificing their family life in pursuit of career success, believing that their efforts will eventually lead to happiness. However, this often results in burnout, strained relationships, and a sense of emptiness despite professional accomplishments.

Work-life balance is not about choosing between career and family—it's about integrating both in a way that allows you to thrive in all areas of life. By maintaining this balance, you not only improve your well-being but also create a positive environment for your family and colleagues. Here are some key strategies to help you achieve this balance effectively.

1. Setting Boundaries for Work and Home Life

To truly succeed in both business and family life, you must set clear boundaries. This means designating specific time for your family without work interruptions. Whether it's having dinner together, attending important events, or simply setting aside time for meaningful conversations, these moments create a sense of connection and reinforce the importance of family.

One common mistake is allowing work to encroach on personal time through emails, calls, and after-hours meetings. While occasional work emergencies are inevitable, making a habit of prioritizing work over family leads to disconnection and resentment. Setting firm boundaries—such as not checking emails after a certain time or dedicating weekends to family activities—ensures that your loved ones receive the time and attention they deserve.

Practical Ways to Set Boundaries

- Establish specific work hours and stick to them.

- Create a separate workspace at home to prevent work from spilling into family life.

- Communicate with your employer or clients about your availability.

- Plan family activities in advance to ensure dedicated time together.

- Set your phone aside during family time to avoid distractions.

When you prioritize uninterrupted family time, you not only strengthen your relationships but also recharge mentally, allowing you to be more effective in your professional life.

2. Being Present, Not Just Physically There

Many professionals struggle with the habit of being physically present but mentally distracted. Simply being home does not equate to quality time if your mind is occupied with emails, deadlines, and business concerns. Your family needs your full presence—your attention, engagement, and emotional availability.

When you actively listen to your loved ones, show appreciation, and participate in family activities, you strengthen the bonds that provide emotional support and happiness. Children, in particular, benefit greatly from having engaged parents who take the time to understand their thoughts and experiences.

Ways to Be More Present in Family Life

- **Practice active listening.** When talking to family members, put away distractions and focus entirely on the conversation.

- **Create tech-free zones.** Designate areas or times in your home where phones, laptops, and work discussions are not allowed.

- **Engage in shared activities.** Whether it's playing games, cooking together, or taking a walk, these moments create lasting memories.

- **Express appreciation.** A simple "thank you," or words of encouragement can go a long way in nurturing strong family relationships.

Being truly present enriches family life and helps you develop deeper, more meaningful connections with your loved ones.

3. Leading by Example

If you have employees, business partners, or colleagues who look up to you, the way you handle your personal life can set a powerful example. A leader who prioritizes family and well-being inspires others to do the same. This fosters a work culture where employees feel empowered to maintain a healthy balance, reducing burnout and increasing overall workplace satisfaction.

Workplaces that encourage work-life balance often have happier, more productive employees. When leaders demonstrate that success does not require sacrificing family life, they create a healthier and more sustainable professional environment.

Encouraging Work-Life Balance in the Workplace

- Support flexible working hours to accommodate family needs.

- Encourage employees to take their vacation days and disconnect from work when off duty.

- Promote a culture that values productivity over long hours.

- Recognize and celebrate employees' personal milestones, such as birthdays and family achievements.

A workplace that respects work-life balance leads to greater employee loyalty, better mental health, and overall higher job satisfaction.

4. The Role of Family in Personal and Professional Growth

Your family is more than just a support system; they play an active role in shaping your character, values, and resilience. Strong family relationships contribute to both personal fulfillment and professional success.

Emotional Support During Challenges

No matter how successful you are, there will be moments when work becomes overwhelming. Having a supportive family to lean on can make all the difference. They provide encouragement, perspective, and motivation when you face setbacks or self-doubt.

Inspiration and Motivation

Many professionals are driven by the desire to provide a better life for their families. Whether it's ensuring financial security, setting an example for children, or creating a legacy, family can be a powerful motivator to push through difficulties and strive for excellence.

Personal Development Through Relationships

Interacting with family teaches important life skills such as patience, empathy, and effective communication. These skills translate directly into the workplace, making you a better leader, teammate, and decision-maker.

5. Prioritizing Self-Care for a Healthier Balance

A common misconception is that maintaining a work-life balance means constantly putting others first. While family and work responsibilities are important, self-care should not be neglected. You cannot effectively care for others or perform well at work if you are physically and emotionally drained.

Self-care includes:

- **Physical health** – Regular exercise, proper nutrition, and sufficient sleep.
- **Mental well-being** – Taking breaks, practicing mindfulness, and seeking support when needed.
- **Personal fulfillment** – Engaging in hobbies, pursuing interests, and spending time on activities that bring joy.

When you take care of yourself, you bring more energy, patience, and positivity into both your family and work life.

6. The Long-Term Benefits of Work-Life Balance

Achieving a balance between work and family is not just about short-term happiness; it has long-term benefits that affect every aspect of life.

Stronger Family Bonds

When you invest time and effort into your family, relationships grow deeper. Stronger bonds lead to a more fulfilling personal life, greater emotional security, and lasting memories with loved ones.

Greater Professional Success

Balanced individuals tend to be more focused, creative, and effective at work. They avoid burnout and make better decisions, leading to long-term career growth and success.

A Healthier and Happier Life

Chronic stress from an unbalanced life can lead to serious health issues. Prioritizing balance helps reduce stress, improve overall well-being, and increase longevity.

Work-life balance is not a luxury—it is a necessity for long-term success and happiness. By setting clear boundaries, being fully present with your family, leading by example, and prioritizing self-care, you can create a fulfilling life that nurtures both personal and professional achievements.

PRACTICAL STEPS TO STRENGTHEN FAMILY BONDS AND ENHANCE SUCCESS

Prioritize Communication

Open and honest communication is the foundation of any strong relationship. Just as in business, assumptions and unspoken frustrations can lead to misunderstandings in family life. Make it a habit to check in with your loved ones regularly, listen actively, and express appreciation.

Schedule Family Time as You Would Business Meetings

Many professionals meticulously schedule their work commitments but leave family time to chance. Just as you plan for important business meetings, schedule dedicated time for your family. Whether it's a weekly outing, a vacation, or a simple game night, these planned moments strengthen relationships.

Practice Self-Care

Your ability to show up as your best self for both your family and your career depends on your personal well-being. Make time for activities that recharge you—exercise, meditation, hobbies, or simply rest. When you take care of yourself, you have more energy to invest in both your family and your work.

Express Gratitude Regularly

Gratitude has the power to shift perspectives and strengthen relationships. Make it a habit to express appreciation not only to your family but also to your colleagues and employees. A culture of gratitude enhances both personal and professional environments.

Recognize That Success Is a Journey, Not a Destination

True success is not about reaching a single milestone—it's about building a life that is fulfilling in all areas. Prioritizing family happiness alongside professional ambition creates a sustainable path where you can enjoy the fruits of your labor without regret.

The most successful people in the world understand that their achievements are deeply connected to the strength of their personal relationships. A fulfilling home life is not just a luxury—it is an essential ingredient for long-term professional success. By investing in your family's happiness, you are not only enriching your personal life but also setting yourself up for greater focus, resilience, and achievement in your career.

Remember, you don't have to choose between personal fulfillment and professional success. The two are interconnected, and when nurtured together, they create a life of true accomplishment and joy.

Examples of Happiness vs. Simplicity in Real Life

"It is very simple to be happy, but it is very difficult to be simple."

Rabindranath Tagore

1. The Overwhelmed Executive

A successful corporate executive, Mr. Sharma, is constantly chasing promotions, accolades, and material wealth. Despite his achievements, he feels a persistent emptiness. One day, he attends a meditation retreat where he learns to appreciate the present moment and the simple joys of life. He realizes that happiness doesn't lie in external accomplishments but in inner peace and simplicity. However, adopting this new mindset proves difficult as he struggles to let go of his competitive nature and the complexities of his high-powered career.

2. The Urban Nomad

Lena, a young tech professional, decides to give up her city apartment to live as a digital nomad, seeking a simpler life. She travels to various countries, working remotely from beaches and mountains. At first, the freedom is intoxicating, and she feels the joy of escaping the chaos of urban life. But as time goes on, she faces the loneliness and unpredictability of a transient lifestyle, realizing that simplicity, while liberating, often requires facing deeper internal struggles about connection and purpose.

3. The Retired Librarian's Reflection

Mr. Thompson, a retired librarian from a small Midwestern town, spends his days tending to his garden and reading classic novels. He enjoys the peaceful rhythm of his life, filled with simple pleasures.

He often shares stories of his busy work life with his grandchildren, telling them how the joy of helping others learn was the truest form of happiness. Looking back, he sees how difficult it was to find simplicity in his younger years, when he juggled a demanding career and personal ambitions. Now, he treasures the uncomplicated beauty of his quiet days.

CHAPTER 3

HAPPINESS AS THE KEY TO HEALTH AND SIMPLICITY

Happiness is often viewed as an elusive goal—something to chase after once success, wealth, or external circumstances align. However, true happiness is not a distant reward; it is a state of being that influences every aspect of your life, from your health to your decision-making. When you cultivate happiness, you gain clarity, resilience, and the ability to focus on what truly matters.

In today's fast-paced world, many people find themselves overwhelmed by stress, endless responsibilities, and unnecessary complications. They believe that success requires struggle, that health is achieved through discipline alone, and that fulfillment comes only after years of sacrifice. But what if the foundation of both well-being and success is much simpler? What if the secret lies in something as fundamental as happiness?

Happiness is not just an emotional state; it is a driving force that shapes your mind, body, and choices. It gives you the energy to thrive, the clarity to simplify your life, and the resilience to overcome obstacles. When you are happy, you make better decisions, your body functions optimally, and life itself becomes easier to navigate.

This chapter explores the powerful connection between happiness, health, and simplicity, showing you how embracing joy can lead to a more fulfilling and successful life.

THE SCIENCE OF HAPPINESS AND HEALTH

It is no coincidence that happy people tend to live longer, have lower stress levels, and maintain better overall health. Research in psychology and neuroscience has repeatedly shown that happiness has a direct impact on physical well-being. When you experience joy, your body releases beneficial chemicals such as endorphins, serotonin, and dopamine—all of which contribute to reduced stress, lower blood pressure, and a stronger immune system.

On the other hand, chronic stress, negativity, and unhappiness can lead to a cascade of health issues, including heart disease, weakened immunity, and mental fatigue. Stress triggers the release of cortisol, a hormone that, when elevated for long periods, can weaken the body's ability to heal and fight illness.

Happiness acts as a natural antidote to stress. When you cultivate a positive mindset, you shift your body's internal chemistry toward balance and well-being. Your heart rate stabilizes, your sleep improves, and your body becomes more resilient to external pressures. Simply put, prioritizing happiness is one of the most effective ways to maintain both mental and physical health.

HAPPINESS BRINGS CLARITY AND SIMPLICITY

When you are unhappy, life feels chaotic. Small problems seem overwhelming, decisions feel complicated, and even simple tasks can become exhausting. But when you are genuinely happy, everything becomes clearer. You focus on what truly matters, letting go of unnecessary worries and distractions.

Happiness allows you to simplify your life in profound ways:

1. Clear Priorities

When you are happy, you no longer feel the need to chase after every opportunity or prove yourself through excessive work. Instead, you prioritize what aligns with your values rather than making choices out of fear, obligation, or societal pressure. Happiness helps you recognize that success is not about accumulating achievements or possessions but about living a life that feels meaningful to you.

People often confuse busyness with productivity, but true fulfillment comes from dedicating time and energy to things that genuinely matter. Happiness allows you to say no to unnecessary commitments and distractions, creating space for personal growth, relationships, and well-being.

2. Better Decision-Making

A happy mind is a clear mind. When you are in a positive state, you are less likely to overthink, second-guess yourself, or make impulsive choices driven by stress. Instead, you make decisions with confidence and clarity.

When you are stressed or unhappy, fear often takes control of your decision-making process. You may find yourself worrying about worst-case scenarios or making choices based on anxiety rather than logic. However, happiness shifts your mindset. It helps you see opportunities instead of obstacles and solutions instead of problems. As a result, your decisions become more intentional and effective.

For example, when choosing between two career paths, an unhappy person might focus on fears—what if I fail? What if I disappoint others? A happy person, on the other hand, will focus on what excites them and what aligns with their long-term goals, leading to a choice based on passion rather than pressure.

3. Less Clutter, More Focus

Emotional well-being encourages a simpler, more intentional lifestyle. Happiness naturally removes complexity from life, making it easier to focus on meaningful goals and relationships.

This extends beyond emotional clutter to physical and mental clutter as well. When you are unhappy, you may seek distractions—overcommitting to obligations, accumulating unnecessary possessions, or filling your schedule to avoid dealing with emotions. However, happiness brings a sense of peace and contentment, making it easier to let go of things that do not serve you.

A simpler life does not mean a lack of ambition or excitement; rather, it means focusing on what truly fulfills you. You stop accumulating unnecessary responsibilities and possessions, choosing instead to invest in experiences, relationships, and self-improvement.

Happiness naturally removes complexity from life, making it easier to focus on meaningful goals and relationships.

THE ROLE OF GRATITUDE IN SUSTAINING HAPPINESS

One of the simplest yet most powerful ways to cultivate happiness is through gratitude. When you focus on what you have instead of what you lack, your perspective shifts. Gratitude rewires your brain to recognize and appreciate the positive aspects of life, reinforcing a mindset of abundance and fulfillment. It allows you to find joy in everyday moments and helps you build resilience in difficult times.

Gratitude is not just about feeling thankful when things go well—it is about maintaining a deep sense of appreciation even during challenges. When faced with hardships, those who practice gratitude are more likely to find silver linings and lessons in their experiences rather than dwelling on negativity. This mental shift reduces stress, strengthens emotional well-being, and increases overall life satisfaction.

Studies in psychology and neuroscience have shown that practicing gratitude activates the brain's reward system, releasing dopamine and serotonin—the "feel-good" chemicals that contribute to happiness. Regular gratitude practice has been linked to lower levels of anxiety and depression, improved sleep quality, and a stronger immune system. In essence, gratitude is not just a mindset; it is a tool for improving mental and physical health.

SIMPLE WAYS TO INCORPORATE GRATITUDE INTO DAILY LIFE

Practicing gratitude does not require grand gestures—it is about developing small, consistent habits that reinforce a positive outlook. Some effective ways to cultivate gratitude include:

1. **Keeping a Gratitude Journal:** Each day, take a few moments to write down three things you are grateful for. These could be simple things, like a warm cup of coffee in the morning, a kind word from a friend, or the feeling of sunshine on your face. Over time, this practice trains your brain to seek and appreciate the positive aspects of life.

2. **Expressing Appreciation to Others:** Gratitude strengthens relationships. A simple "thank you" to a loved one, colleague, or even a stranger can create deeper connections and spread positivity. Try writing thank-you notes, sending thoughtful messages, or verbally acknowledging the kindness of others.

3. **Starting the Day with Gratitude:** Before getting out of bed each morning, take a moment to reflect on at least one thing you are grateful for. This sets a positive tone for the day and helps shift your focus toward abundance rather than stress.

4. **Reframing Negative Experiences:** When faced with challenges, ask yourself, *What can I learn from this?* Or *Is*

there something positive hidden in this situation? This shift in perspective helps cultivate resilience and optimism.

5. **Mindful Gratitude Practice:** Throughout the day, pause and acknowledge the good things around you—the laughter of a child, the beauty of nature, or a moment of peace. Practicing mindfulness in this way allows you to fully appreciate life's simple joys.

LETTING GO OF NEGATIVITY AND OVERCOMPLICATION

Negativity often stems from holding onto things that no longer serve you—whether it's past disappointments, toxic relationships, or unnecessary commitments. Many people make life harder than it needs to be by overcomplicating situations, obsessing over minor details, or carrying emotional baggage from the past.

To embrace happiness and simplicity, learn to:

- **Release grudges and resentment** – Holding onto negative emotions only drains your energy. Forgiveness does not mean excusing wrongs, but freeing yourself from the burden of anger.

- **Say no to unnecessary stress** – Not every opportunity is worth pursuing, and not every problem is yours to solve. Learning to set boundaries is a crucial step toward a happier life.

- **Declutter your physical and mental space** – A cluttered environment often leads to a cluttered mind. Simplifying your surroundings and commitments can lead to greater peace and clarity.

Letting go of negativity makes room for joy, creativity, and a sense of ease in your daily life.

HAPPINESS IS A CHOICE, NOT A DESTINATION

Many people believe that happiness will come after they achieve a certain goal—whether it's financial success, career advancement, or personal milestones. But happiness is not something to be postponed. It is a mindset and a choice you can make every day.

Rather than waiting for happiness to arrive, cultivate it in the present by:

- **Finding joy in small moments** – A beautiful sunrise, a heartfelt conversation, or a simple act of kindness can bring immense joy if you take the time to appreciate it.

- **Prioritizing relationships** – Genuine connections with family, friends, and colleagues contribute more to happiness than material success ever could.

- **Practicing mindfulness** – Being present in the moment prevents you from dwelling on past regrets or future anxieties. Mindfulness helps you embrace life as it unfolds.

The more you choose happiness, the more it becomes a natural part of your life.

CONCLUSION: A LIFE OF HAPPINESS AND SIMPLICITY

Happiness is the foundation for a healthy, simple, and fulfilling life. It strengthens your body, sharpens your mind, and simplifies your decisions. By choosing joy, letting go of negativity, and embracing gratitude, you create a life that is not only successful but deeply rewarding.

Simplicity follows happiness naturally—when you focus on what truly matters, unnecessary complexity fades away. You become more present, more purposeful, and more at peace with yourself and the world around you.

Happiness is not an external achievement; it is an internal state. And the moment you make it a priority, everything else—health, clarity, success—falls into place.

Stories of Clarity and Joy

"Happiness is not something ready-made. It comes from your own actions."

- Dalai Lama

---

1. The Content Farmer – Finding Joy in Simplicity

Li Wei had inherited a large rice farm from his father in a quiet village in southern China. While his neighbors rushed to modernize with heavy machinery and chemical fertilizers, Li Wei chose a simpler path. He farmed the way his ancestors had for generations—using natural compost, rotating crops, and relying on traditional wisdom to maintain the land's health.

One year, a devastating drought hit the region. Many farms suffered heavy losses, and their soil cracked and barren. But Li Wei's land, carefully nurtured with sustainable methods, retained moisture better than most. His harvest, though modest, was enough to sustain him and his family.

When asked why he didn't chase higher profits like others, Li Wei smiled and said, "I don't measure success by the size of my harvest, but by the peace in my heart. A simple life with happiness is far richer than a complicated life with stress."

2. The Grateful Nurse – Health Through Happiness

Sophia had been a nurse for over two decades. She had seen patients who were physically strong yet fell apart under stress, while others, despite their ailments, remained joyful and lived longer than expected. Over time, she noticed a pattern—patients who maintained a positive outlook often recovered faster.

One day, she was assigned to an elderly woman, Mrs. Thompson, who had been given a dire prognosis. But instead of dwelling on her illness, Mrs. Thompson filled her days with laughter, gratitude, and love. Against all odds, she lived much longer than doctors predicted.

Inspired, Sophia adopted a new approach to life. She no longer carried stress home from work and made happiness a priority in her own life. She often reminded her colleagues, "A joyful heart heals faster than medicine ever can."

3. The Forgiving Friend – Letting Go for Inner Peace

Lisa and her best friend, Hannah, had been inseparable since childhood. But one day, a misunderstanding led to a bitter argument. Years passed without a word between them, and Lisa held onto resentment.

One evening, Lisa attended a seminar about the power of happiness. The speaker said, "Holding onto anger is like drinking poison and expecting the other person to suffer." That night, Lisa realized she had been carrying unnecessary negativity.

She reached out to Hannah, and to her surprise, Hannah had wanted to reconnect, too. The weight Lisa had carried for years disappeared in an instant. She learned that forgiveness is not about making the other person feel better—it's about freeing yourself.

Each of these stories reveals a truth: happiness is not something you wait for—it's something you choose. By embracing joy, gratitude, simplicity, and forgiveness, you create a life that is not only healthier and more fulfilling but also more meaningful.

A happy life is not built on wealth, status, or external validation—it is built on your ability to appreciate the present, make space for what truly matters, and let go of what does not serve you.

CHAPTER 4

OUR BODY: A PERFECT MACHINE

Imagine owning the most advanced, high-performing machine in the world—one capable of adapting, healing, and functioning in perfect harmony with its surroundings. Now, realize that you already do. That machine is your body. Unlike any man-made invention, the human body is a self-sustaining, incredibly efficient system designed for endurance, resilience, and peak performance. However, like any finely tuned machine, it requires regular maintenance, care, and attention to function at its best.

Too often, people neglect their bodies, expecting them to keep running despite a lack of proper fuel, rest, and upkeep. Just as you wouldn't expect a car to run forever without oil changes or a computer to function flawlessly without software updates, you can't expect your body to perform at its highest level without care. The good news is that maintaining this incredible machine isn't complicated—it just requires consistency and balance in both physical and mental well-being.

FUELING YOUR BODY—THE ROLE OF NUTRITION

Every machine needs the right fuel, and your body is no different. What you consume directly impacts how well your body functions, how much energy you have, and even how clearly you think. The food and drink choices you make today determine how well your body will serve you in the long run. If you prioritize high-quality nutrition, you can enhance your physical and mental performance, prevent diseases, and maintain a balanced lifestyle.

1. Eat to Perform, Not Just to Survive

Many people eat out of habit or convenience rather than for nourishment. Highly processed foods, excess sugar, and unhealthy fats clog the system, leading to sluggishness, poor concentration, and long-term health issues such as obesity, diabetes, and cardiovascular disease. On the other hand, a diet rich in whole foods—lean proteins, healthy fats, fiber, and essential vitamins—keeps your body operating efficiently and your mind sharp.

Think of food as fuel for your body:

- **High-quality fuel** (fruits, vegetables, whole grains, lean proteins, and healthy fats) keeps your system clean and running smoothly, promoting energy, clear thinking, and strong immunity.

- **Low-quality fuel** (processed foods, sugary drinks, refined carbohydrates, and trans fats) slows down your body's functions and leads to breakdowns over time, making you more prone to fatigue, brain fog, and chronic illnesses.

Instead of focusing on restrictive diets or eliminating entire food groups, prioritize balance and variety. The goal is to nourish your body with natural, nutrient-dense foods that provide lasting energy rather than quick but temporary highs.

Macronutrients: The Building Blocks of Energy

To function optimally, your body requires a balanced intake of macronutrients:

- **Proteins** – Essential for muscle repair, growth, and overall cellular function. Good sources include lean meats, poultry, fish, eggs, beans, lentils, nuts, and dairy products.

- **Carbohydrates** – The body's primary energy source. Whole grains, fruits, and vegetables provide complex carbs, which release energy gradually and keep you fueled

42

longer. Processed carbohydrates, like white bread and pastries, spike blood sugar and lead to energy crashes.

- **Fats** – Healthy fats are crucial for brain function, hormone regulation, and energy storage. Focus on sources like avocados, nuts, seeds, olive oil, and fatty fish while avoiding trans fats found in fried and processed foods.

Micronutrients: The Small but Mighty Essentials

Vitamins and minerals are just as important as macronutrients. They support metabolism, immune function, and overall well-being. Some key micronutrients include:

- **Vitamin C** (found in citrus fruits and bell peppers) for immune support.

- **Iron** (from leafy greens, beans, and lean meats) for energy production.

- **Calcium** (from dairy, almonds, and leafy greens) for strong bones.

- **Magnesium** (from nuts, seeds, and whole grains) for muscle function and stress management.

Eating a variety of colorful, unprocessed foods ensures that your body gets the necessary vitamins and minerals to function at its best.

2. Hydration—The Lifeblood of Your System

Water is to your body what oil is to an engine. Without it, everything slows down. Dehydration doesn't just make you thirsty—it can cause fatigue, brain fog, muscle cramps, dizziness, and a weakened immune system. Proper hydration plays a role in almost every bodily function, including digestion, circulation, and temperature regulation.

Why Staying Hydrated Matters

- **Flushes Out Toxins** – Water helps remove waste products from the body, supporting kidney function and overall detoxification.

- **Boosts Energy Levels** – Even mild dehydration can lead to feelings of tiredness and sluggishness. Drinking enough water ensures that oxygen and nutrients are effectively transported to your cells.

- **Supports Digestion** – Water aids in breaking down food and absorbing nutrients efficiently, preventing bloating and constipation.

- **Enhances Brain Function** – Your brain is nearly 75% water. Staying hydrated improves concentration, memory, and mental clarity.

How Much Water Do You Really Need?

A general rule of thumb is to drink at least eight glasses (64 ounces) of water per day, but individual needs vary based on activity level, climate, and body size. If you exercise regularly or live in a hot environment, you may need more.

A simple habit to adopt: Carry a reusable water bottle with you and sip throughout the day. Setting reminders on your phone or using a hydration-tracking app can help ensure you're drinking enough water.

To enhance hydration, consider infusing your water with fresh fruits, cucumbers, or mint for a natural flavor boost. Coconut water and herbal teas are also excellent hydration sources. However, avoid sugary sodas and excessive caffeine, as they can contribute to dehydration rather than preventing it.

3. Smart Eating Habits for Long-Term Health

Good nutrition isn't just about what you eat—it's also about **how you eat**. Developing mindful eating habits can improve digestion, prevent overeating, and help you develop a healthier relationship with food.

1. Eat Mindfully: Instead of rushing through meals or eating in front of a screen, focus on the **experience of eating**. Chew your food slowly, savor the flavors, and listen to your body's hunger and fullness cues.

2. Plan Your Meals: Planning meals ahead of time reduces the likelihood of making unhealthy, impulsive food choices. Preparing nutritious snacks and meals in advance ensures that you always have access to healthy options, even on busy days.

3. Don't Skip Meals: Skipping meals, especially breakfast, can lead to **energy crashes and overeating later in the day**. Start your morning with a balanced meal that includes protein, healthy fats, and fiber to keep your metabolism steady and your energy levels high.

4. Control Portion Sizes: Even healthy foods can lead to weight gain if consumed in excessive amounts. Use smaller plates, serve appropriate portion sizes, and avoid eating straight from large packages to prevent overeating.

5. Limit Sugar and Processed Foods: Excessive sugar intake can cause spikes and crashes in blood sugar levels, leading to cravings and mood swings. Replace sugary snacks with healthier alternatives like nuts, yogurt, or fruit to maintain stable energy throughout the day.

EXERCISE—KEEPING THE MACHINE IN MOTION

A well-maintained machine needs to stay in motion to avoid rust and deterioration. Your body is no different. Regular physical activity strengthens muscles, boosts endurance, and keeps your internal systems functioning optimally.

1. Move with Purpose

You don't have to spend hours in a gym to stay fit. The key is to move intentionally every day:

- Take the stairs instead of the elevator.
- Walk or bike instead of driving short distances.
- Stretch throughout the day to release tension and improve flexibility.

Exercise is not about punishment—it's about keeping your body in top condition so you can enjoy life to the fullest.

2. Strength, Endurance, and Flexibility—The Three Pillars of Fitness

A strong body isn't just about lifting heavy weights. It requires a balance of:

- **Strength training** to build muscle and improve metabolism.
- **Cardiovascular exercise** to enhance heart and lung health.
- **Flexibility exercises** like yoga or stretching to maintain mobility and prevent injuries.

Find activities that you enjoy—dancing, swimming, hiking, or even playing with your kids. When movement becomes fun, consistency follows naturally.

REST AND RECOVERY—THE MACHINE NEEDS DOWNTIME

Even the best machines need time to cool down and reset to function at peak performance. Your body is no different. Rest and recovery are not just luxuries; they are essential components of overall well-being. When you neglect proper rest, you put yourself at risk of burnout, weakened immunity, and decreased mental and physical performance.

Think of a high-performance car—without regular maintenance and cool-down periods, its engine overheats, parts wear out faster, and performance declines. The same principle applies to your body. When you don't allow it enough time to repair, rebuild, and recharge, you'll experience fatigue, reduced endurance, and difficulty concentrating.

Incorporating quality sleep, active recovery, and intentional relaxation into your routine ensures that your body and mind stay in top condition, ready to tackle daily challenges with energy and clarity.

1. The Power of Sleep

Sleep is the ultimate reset button for your body. A well-rested body and mind perform significantly better than one running on exhaustion. While you sleep, your body:

- **Repairs tissues** – Muscle growth, cell regeneration, and immune system strengthening all happen during deep sleep.

- **Consolidates memories** – Your brain processes and stores information, helping you learn and retain new skills.

- **Restores energy** – Sleep replenishes energy stores and regulates metabolism.

When sleep is cut short, all of these essential processes are *disrupted*, leading to reduced physical and mental performance, increased stress levels, and a greater risk of chronic illnesses like heart disease and diabetes.

Adults should aim for *7-9 hours of sleep per night* to function at their best. However, it's not just about the quantity of sleep—it's also about the quality. Poor-quality sleep can leave you feeling just as drained as not sleeping at all.

47

If you experience any of the following regularly, your body is likely crying out for more rest:

- Feeling tired even after a full night's sleep
- Difficulty focusing or remembering things
- Mood swings and irritability
- Increased cravings for sugary or high-carb foods
- Frequent colds or a weakened immune system

Simple Tips to Improve Sleep Quality

Good sleep hygiene can make all the difference in getting deep, restorative rest. Try incorporating these proven strategies:

- **Keep a Regular Sleep Schedule** – Go to bed and wake up at the same time every day, even on weekends. A consistent routine regulates your body's internal clock.

- **Avoid Screens Before Bed** – The blue light from phones, tablets, and TVs interferes with melatonin production, the hormone that helps you fall asleep. Power down at least *30-60 minutes* before bedtime.

- **Create a Bedtime Routine** – Establish relaxing pre-sleep habits, such as reading, stretching, or practicing deep breathing. This signals to your body that it's time to wind down.

- **Optimize Your Sleep Environment** – Keep your bedroom *cool, dark,* and *quiet.* Invest in a comfortable mattress and pillows.

- **Limit Caffeine and Alcohol Before Bed** – Stimulants like caffeine disrupt sleep, while alcohol can interfere with deep sleep cycles. Try to avoid them at least *4-6 hours* before bedtime.

By prioritizing sleep, you enhance brain function, boost physical performance, and improve overall well-being. Sleep isn't a waste of time - it's an investment in your health.

2. Active Recovery Matters

Rest isn't just about sleep—it also includes *active recovery*, the process of restoring your body through movement, relaxation, and stress reduction. While sleep is passive recovery, active recovery keeps your body engaged while allowing it to heal and rejuvenate.

When you engage in physical activity, your muscles experience tiny tears and stress. Active recovery helps repair and strengthen muscles, preventing soreness and injury. Additionally, stress and tension accumulate throughout the day, and active recovery techniques help release that tension, reducing mental fatigue.

Types of Active Recovery

- **Stretching** – Helps relieve muscle tightness, improves flexibility, and prevents injuries.

- **Yoga** – Combines gentle movement with breath control, reducing stress and improving circulation.

- **Meditation & Deep Breathing** – Lowers stress hormones, relaxes the nervous system, and improves mental clarity.

- **Low-Intensity Exercise** – Activities like walking, swimming, or cycling at a slow pace promote blood circulation and aid muscle recovery.

- **Foam Rolling & Massage** – Helps break up muscle knots, increase circulation, and reduce soreness.

Even if you don't have time for a full workout or meditation session, taking just 10 minutes for active recovery can recharge your energy levels. Try this simple routine:

1. **Stretch for 2-3 minutes** – Focus on your shoulders, neck, and back if you've been sitting for long hours.

2. **Take deep breaths for 1-2 minutes** – Inhale deeply for four counts, hold for four, and exhale for four. This instantly calms your nervous system.

3. **Go for a short walk** – Even a quick stroll around your home or office can increase circulation and improve focus.

4. **Perform light movements** – A few squats, arm circles, or gentle yoga poses can help wake up your muscles.

Making active recovery a daily habit prevents burnout, keeps your body resilient, and ensures you perform at your best in all areas of life.

3. The Role of Mental Rest

Just as your body needs downtime, your mind also needs rest. Mental fatigue is just as real as physical fatigue, and if left unchecked, it can lead to brain fog, stress, anxiety, and burnout.

Below are some signs of mental exhaustion:

- Struggling to focus or remember things
- Feeling easily overwhelmed by simple tasks
- Frequent headaches or tension in the body
- Irritability or lack of motivation

How to Give Your Mind a Break

- **Practice Mindfulness** – Take short breaks throughout the day to breathe, reflect, or step away from your tasks.
- **Engage in a Hobby** – Doing something you enjoy, like painting, playing music, or reading, helps shift your focus and refreshes your mind.

- **Unplug from Technology** – Constant notifications and screen time drain mental energy. Schedule tech-free time to reset.

- **Spend Time Outdoors** – Nature has been proven to reduce stress and improve mood. A short walk outside can work wonders.

- **Prioritize Downtime** – Don't feel guilty about taking breaks. Rest is not laziness—it's an essential part of maintaining long-term productivity and well-being.

Remember: The better you take care of your body, the better it will take care of you.

MINDSET—THE MENTAL OPERATING SYSTEM

A machine is only as effective as its software, and your mind serves as the operating system of your body. No matter how well a machine is maintained, if the software is outdated or corrupted, the entire system suffers. Likewise, physical health alone isn't enough - your mental well-being plays an equally important role in keeping your body functioning optimally. A strong, resilient mind leads to better choices, greater emotional stability, and the ability to navigate life's challenges with clarity and confidence.

By cultivating the right mindset, you can unlock your full potential, improve your overall well-being, and create a harmonious balance between body and mind.

1. The Power of Mindfulness

Mindfulness - the practice of being fully present and engaged in the moment - is one of the most powerful tools for improving mental and physical health. When you practice mindfulness, you train your brain to focus, reduce stress, and make intentional choices, all of which contribute to a healthier lifestyle.

Studies have shown that practicing mindfulness lowers cortisol levels (the stress hormone), reduces anxiety, and improves sleep. It also enhances the brain's ability to regulate emotions, leading to better decision-making and a more positive outlook on life.

When you are mindful, you make healthier choices about food, exercise, and overall well-being. Instead of reacting impulsively or turning to unhealthy habits, you learn to pause, reflect, and respond with awareness.

Simple Ways to Practice Mindfulness

You don't need to meditate for hours or attend a retreat to practice mindfulness. It can be integrated into everyday activities with simple habits like:

- **Taking deep breaths when feeling overwhelmed** – Deep breathing activates the parasympathetic nervous system, calming your body and mind.

- **Eating meals slowly and appreciating flavors** – Instead of rushing through your meals, savor each bite and listen to your body's hunger and fullness cues.

- **Focusing on the present moment rather than worrying about the past or future** – Let go of regrets and future anxieties by bringing your attention back to what is happening now.

- **Engaging fully in tasks** – Whether it's exercising, working, or having a conversation, give it your full attention without distractions.

- **Spending time in nature** – Walking in a park, feeling the sun on your skin, or listening to the sounds of nature can instantly ground you in the present moment.

Mindfulness isn't just good for your *mental well-being* - it directly affects your *physical health* too. By reducing stress, it helps lower blood pressure, improve digestion, strengthen the immune system, and even speed up recovery from illness or injury. When your mind is at peace, your body functions more efficiently.

2. Positive Self-Talk—Reprogramming Your Mind

Just as a computer can be programmed with either helpful or harmful code, your mind is shaped by the words you tell yourself. If your inner dialogue is full of negativity, doubt, and self-criticism, it can limit your potential, drain your energy, and even manifest as physical symptoms like fatigue, tension, and stress. However, if you practice positive self-talk, you can rewire your brain to become stronger, more confident, and more resilient.

Your body listens to what your mind believes. If you constantly tell yourself:

- "I'm not good enough."
- "I'm too tired to work out."
- "I'll never be healthy."

Your brain accepts these statements as truth, and your body responds accordingly. You feel more fatigued, less motivated, and stuck in unhealthy habits.

To shift your mindset, replace negative thoughts with empowering statements:

- "I am strong and capable."
- "I deserve to be healthy and happy."
- "Every small step I take brings me closer to my best self."
- "I am in control of my choices and my future."

Practical Ways to Implement Positive Self-Talk

1. **Catch Yourself** – The first step to changing your mindset is noticing negative thoughts when they arise. Pay attention to your inner dialogue throughout the day.

2. **Flip the Script** – When you catch yourself thinking something negative, immediately reframe it into something positive. Instead of saying, "I can't do this," try, "I am learning and improving every day."

3. **Use Daily Affirmations** – Start your morning with affirmations like "I am grateful for my body," "I radiate confidence," or "I make choices that support my well-being."

4. **Surround Yourself with Positivity** – The environment around you influences your mindset. Listen to uplifting music, read motivational books, and spend time with supportive, positive people.

5. **Visualize Success** – Picture yourself achieving your goals, whether it's running a marathon, overcoming a challenge, or simply feeling happier and healthier. Visualization **reinforces** the belief that you can succeed.

Your thoughts don't just affect your emotions—they directly impact your physical health. Research shows that people who maintain a positive outlook experience:

- **Lower stress levels** – Reducing chronic stress can prevent high blood pressure, heart disease, and other health issues.

- **Stronger immune systems** – Optimistic individuals are less likely to get sick and recover faster from illnesses.

- **Better pain management** – A positive mindset has been linked to lower pain perception and faster healing.

3. Resilience—Building Mental Strength for Life's Challenges

A strong mind isn't just about thinking positively—it's about developing resilience, the ability to bounce back from setbacks, face challenges with confidence, and adapt to change. Just like a well-built machine can handle wear and tear, a resilient mind can withstand life's difficulties without breaking down.

How to Build Mental Resilience

Embrace Challenges as Learning Opportunities – Instead of fearing failure, see obstacles as stepping stones to growth. Every challenge you overcome makes you stronger.

Develop a Growth Mindset – Believe that your abilities and intelligence can improve with effort and persistence. Avoid saying, "I'm just not good at this." Instead, say, "I can improve with practice."

Practice Gratitude – Focusing on what you have, rather than what you lack, shifts your perspective and increases happiness. Try writing down three things you're grateful for each day.

Take Breaks and Rest – Just like a machine needs downtime for maintenance, your mind needs rest to recharge. Prioritize sleep, relaxation, and self-care.

Surround Yourself with Support – Strong social connections improve mental and physical well-being. Seek out positive, uplifting relationships and avoid negativity whenever possible.

Your mind and body work together—what you think affects how you feel, and how you feel impacts how you function. By cultivating mindfulness, positive self-talk, and resilience, you set yourself up for greater success, better health, and a more fulfilling life.

- A mindful mind makes better choices.

- A positive mind fuels a healthy body.

- A resilient mind can overcome any challenge.

PRACTICAL STRATEGIES TO MAINTAIN THE BODY'S "PERFECT CONDITION"

To keep your body operating at its best, commit to small, daily habits that add up over time. Here's a simple action plan:

1. **Fuel Your Body Wisely** – Eat whole foods, stay hydrated, and nourish yourself with the right nutrients.

2. **Move Every Day** – Find activities you enjoy, whether it's walking, dancing, or weight training.

3. **Prioritize Rest** – Sleep well, take breaks, and allow your body time to recover.

4. **Strengthen Your Mind** – Practice mindfulness, engage in positive self-talk, and manage stress effectively.

5. **Listen to Your Body** – Pay attention to signs of fatigue, stress, or imbalance, and adjust your habits accordingly.

Treat your body like the masterpiece it truly is. Your body is the most advanced, intelligent, and powerful creation you will ever own. When you take care of it, it rewards you with energy, clarity, and resilience. When you neglect it, it struggles to keep up. The choice is yours: maintain your body with care and intention, and it will carry you through a long, fulfilling life. Treat it with the respect it deserves. It's not just a machine; it's the foundation of everything you do. Keep it strong, keep it healthy, and it will serve you well for years to come.

SAVE YOUR HOSPITAL BILL

Alcohol and drugs often promise a brief escape from stress, loneliness, or pain. They provide a temporary high, a fleeting moment of happiness. But what follows is far from pleasant—hangovers, withdrawals, declining health, and, in many cases, addiction. What starts as a casual indulgence can turn into a lifelong burden, both physically and financially.

Studies have shown that excessive alcohol and drug use contribute to chronic illnesses, liver failure, heart disease, and mental health disorders. The money spent on medical treatments, rehabilitation, and emergency care far outweighs the short-lived joy these substances provide. A single night of excess can lead to a lifetime of health complications—and a mountain of medical bills.

A LEGACY OF HEALTH AND RESPONSIBILITY

"When you overcome the temptation, you save it for your next generations." This means that every healthy choice you make today sets an example for the future. Your children, siblings, or younger relatives are watching. If they see you choosing a better path, they're more likely to do the same.

Breaking free from unhealthy habits doesn't just protect your own well-being—it creates a ripple effect. A home free from addiction fosters a healthier environment for the next generation. Instead of passing down medical debts and health struggles, you leave behind a legacy of strength, discipline, and longevity.

Substance abuse often runs in families, not just through genetics but through habits and learned behaviors. If you grew up seeing alcohol as a coping mechanism, you might unconsciously follow that path. But cycles can be broken. Every time you choose to say no to unhealthy temptations, you rewrite the future.

Imagine a future where your children don't have to grow up worrying about a parent's health issues caused by alcohol or drugs. Imagine saving the money spent on hospital visits and putting it toward something meaningful—education, travel, or securing a comfortable life. Choosing health today means saving both your body and your finances from unnecessary harm.

EMPOWERMENT THROUGH EDUCATION

Understanding the real costs of substance abuse—physically, emotionally, and financially—can be life-changing. Alcohol and drugs don't just harm individuals; they impact families, careers, and entire communities. The more you educate yourself on the long-term consequences, the easier it becomes to resist temptation.

Instead of seeking temporary relief through harmful substances, invest in healthier alternatives: exercise, meditation, creative hobbies, or meaningful social connections. The key to lasting happiness isn't found at the bottom of a bottle—it's built through conscious choices that promote well-being.

Health is wealth. The money spent on excessive drinking and drug use often ends up funding hospital bills, treatments, and prescriptions that could have been avoided. By choosing a healthier lifestyle today, you not only save your own future but also inspire others to do the same.

Instead of spending your hard-earned money on hospital visits and costly treatments, invest in your well-being today. Your health is in your hands, and every smart choice you make now saves you from unnecessary suffering later. Save yourself, save your future, and, most importantly—save your hospital bill.

"Take care of your body. It's the only place you have to live."

- Jim Rohn

1. The CEO Who Reclaimed His Life – The Importance of Downtime

For years, Damian was the kind of CEO who thrived on 80-hour workweeks. Vacations? Unthinkable. Breaks? A waste of time. His company grew, but so did his stress, and his health took a hit—constant headaches, anxiety, and near-burnout.

One day, his mentor told him, "A company can't thrive if its leader is running on empty." That advice stuck.

Damian started setting boundaries - no emails after 8 p.m., weekends off, and actual vacations. He expected his team to do the same. The result? His company didn't fall apart. In fact, productivity increased, and for the first time in years, he actually felt alive.

2. The Overworked Doctor – Learning the Power of Sleep

Dr. Raj Mehta was a dedicated surgeon, often working 16-hour shifts at the hospital. His skills were unmatched, but his exhaustion was catching up to him. He told himself he could function on four hours of sleep—after all, he had done it in medical school.

One evening, after finishing back-to-back surgeries, Raj got behind the wheel to drive home. His eyelids were heavy, and he barely remembered the journey. A blaring horn jolted him awake just in time to swerve away from oncoming traffic.

Shaken, he pulled over and sat in silence, realizing how close he had come to disaster. That night, he vowed to prioritize rest—not just for himself, but for his patients. He adjusted his schedule, committed to getting a full night's sleep, and soon noticed the difference. His hands were steadier, his focus sharper, and his energy renewed.

3. The Marathon Runner – Recovery as a Strategy

Ava was training for her first marathon, pushing herself harder each day. She ignored muscle soreness, skipped rest days, and believed that stopping meant weakness.

Then, two weeks before race day, she felt a sharp pain in her knee. The doctor's verdict? A stress injury from overtraining. "If you had given your body time to recover, this wouldn't have happened," he told her.

Frustrated but determined, Ava shifted her mindset. She started incorporating active recovery—yoga, stretching, proper hydration, and rest days—into her training. The next year, when she ran her marathon, she didn't just finish strong—she enjoyed the race.

4. The Artist Who Forgot to Rest – Creative Burnout

For years, Mateo thrived on inspiration, staying up late painting for hours at a time. But one day, his creativity vanished. The more he forced himself to work, the worse it got. He stared at blank canvases, unable to bring his ideas to life.

Desperate for a solution, he took a break—a real one. He went on long walks, spent time with friends, and even traveled to a quiet village for a few weeks. Slowly, the colors returned to his mind.

When he picked up his brush again, his creativity flowed effortlessly. Mateo learned that rest wasn't a break from productivity—it was an essential part of it.

Each of these stories shows the same truth: your body and mind are not designed to run endlessly. Recovery isn't just about avoiding exhaustion - it's about maximizing your potential. By prioritizing sleep, embracing active recovery, and making time for real rest, you don't slow down your progress - you sustain it.

Taking care of yourself isn't about doing less. It's about doing better.

CHAPTER 5

LET GO OF THE PAST AND STAY PRESENT

"You can't start the next chapter of your life if you keep re-reading the last one."

Imagine carrying a heavy backpack everywhere you go. Inside, you've stuffed regrets from the past, worries about the future, and every mistake you've ever made. The weight slows you down, drains your energy, and keeps you from fully experiencing the present. But what if you could put it down?

The past is unchangeable, and the future is uncertain. The only time you can truly influence is the present moment. Yet, many people spend their lives stuck in the past or anxious about the future, missing out on the opportunities right in front of them. When you learn to release what no longer serves you and focus on the here and now, you'll find greater peace, clarity, and joy.

This chapter will guide you through why letting go of the past and staying present is essential, and how you can train your mind to embrace the moment.

WHY HOLDING ONTO THE PAST HOLDS YOU BACK

It's natural to reflect on past experiences. Your memories shape who you are, and lessons from past mistakes help you grow. However, living in the past is different from learning from it.

Dwelling on past mistakes, missed opportunities, or painful events keeps you stuck in a cycle of regret. You replay conversations in your head, wondering what you could have said differently. You beat yourself up for choices you made years ago. You might dwell on relationships that ended, jobs you didn't take, or chances you let slip away. But no amount of thinking can undo what has already happened.

If you're always looking backward, you miss the opportunities that exist right now. Life is constantly moving forward, and staying stuck in the past only holds you back from growth, happiness, and success.

One of the most significant dangers of dwelling on the past is that it distorts your perception of reality. You might romanticize past experiences, believing they were better than they actually were, or exaggerate past failures, making them seem worse than they truly are. This mental trap creates a false comparison, making your present seem dull, disappointing, or hopeless in contrast.

Another issue is how the past affects your self-identity. If you constantly define yourself by past mistakes or painful experiences, you limit your potential. You might tell yourself, I always mess things up, or I can never trust anyone again, reinforcing a cycle that prevents growth. The more you believe these thoughts, the more you live according to them, making it harder to move forward.

The Illusion of Control

One reason people struggle to let go of the past is the illusion of control. You might think, *if only I had done this instead...* or *I should have known better...* These thoughts trick you into believing that if you analyze the past enough, you can change its outcome.

The reality is that no amount of regret, guilt, or overthinking can alter what has already happened. Your mind tries to rewrite history in an attempt to find comfort, but the past is set in stone. What you *can* control is your response to it—how you interpret those experiences and how you allow them to shape your future.

Letting go of this illusion requires shifting your mindset. Instead of focusing on what you *should* have done, ask yourself:

- What have I learned from this experience?

- How can I use this lesson to make better choices today?

- What is one small step I can take right now to move forward?

By redirecting your thoughts from the past to the present, you regain control—not over what has already happened, but over what happens next.

Another aspect of the illusion of control is *seeking closure where there is none.* Sometimes, people hold onto painful memories because they are waiting for an apology, an explanation, or some kind of justice. While closure is desirable, it is not always within your control. Learning to accept incomplete endings is part of emotional freedom. The key is understanding that your healing does not depend on external factors—it depends on your decision to move forward, regardless of whether or not you receive the closure you seek.

The Emotional Toll of Living in the Past

Constantly reliving past failures or heartbreaks doesn't just affect your mood—it impacts your mental, emotional, and physical health. Studies show that dwelling on negative memories:

- **Increases stress levels:** Your brain can't tell the difference between a real threat and a remembered one. Reliving painful events triggers the same stress response as if they were happening now.

- **Raises cortisol levels:** Chronic stress leads to high levels of cortisol, which weakens the immune system, disrupts sleep, and increases the risk of heart disease.

- **Contributes to anxiety and depression:** The more you focus on past mistakes or regrets, the more likely you are to feel hopeless and stuck.

When you live in the past, you also limit your ability to form meaningful connections in the present. For example, someone who carries emotional baggage from a past relationship may struggle to trust new partners, pushing them away before giving the relationship a fair chance. Similarly, if you were hurt by a friend or family member in the past, you might unconsciously expect the same treatment from others, causing you to withdraw or remain guarded.

This emotional burden can also manifest in self-destructive habits, such as procrastination, emotional eating, or avoidance behaviors. If you are constantly weighed down by guilt, regret, or resentment, you may find yourself stuck in unhealthy cycles—staying in toxic relationships, avoiding opportunities out of fear of failure, or sabotaging your own happiness because you feel undeserving.

A key realization is that *holding onto negative emotions doesn't punish the person or event that caused them—it punishes you.* If someone hurt you in the past, your continued suffering does nothing to change them or their actions. It only prolongs your own pain. The more you cling to resentment, anger, or guilt, the more power you give to the very thing that hurt you.

Letting go doesn't mean forgetting or pretending something didn't happen. It means choosing to release the grip the past has on you so you can move forward with clarity and peace. It means choosing to prioritize your own well-being over past hurts.

A helpful exercise is to write down what you're holding onto— whether it's regret, resentment, or guilt—and ask yourself:

65

- How is this serving me?

- Is holding onto this pain helping me, or is it holding me back?

- What would my life look like if I chose to release this burden?

Sometimes, the simple act of recognizing how the past is weighing you down is the first step toward letting it go.

The past is like an old book—there's value in reading it once, but if you keep rereading the same painful chapters, you'll never move forward to the next part of your story.

Your past does not define you—your choices today do. You are not the same person you were then. You have grown, changed, and evolved. The mistakes you made were stepping stones, not life sentences. The people who hurt you do not control your future.

Every day is a new opportunity to create the life you want. Instead of being weighed down by regrets, use the lessons you've learned to build something better.

Let go of what no longer serves you, and embrace the life that's waiting for you *right now.*

THE TRAP OF WORRYING ABOUT THE FUTURE

Just as the past can weigh you down, excessive worry about the future can rob you of peace. While planning and goal-setting are important, fixating on *what-ifs* can leave you feeling anxious and paralyzed.

- What if I fail?

- What if I make the wrong decision?

- What if things don't work out the way I want?

The truth is, no one can predict the future. The more you obsess over things beyond your control, the more overwhelmed you'll feel. Uncertainty is a natural part of life, and learning to embrace it is essential for peace of mind.

Many people believe that worrying about the future helps them prepare, but in reality, excessive worry does the opposite—it drains your energy, clouds your judgment, and stops you from fully engaging in the present. Worrying doesn't give you control over the future; it only steals your joy today.

Imagine carrying a heavy backpack filled with *what-ifs* everywhere you go. The weight of constant worry slows you down, making it difficult to move forward. Now imagine setting that backpack down. Suddenly, you feel lighter, freer, and able to focus on what truly matters—what you can do right now.

Overthinking and Decision Paralysis

Worrying about the future often leads to overthinking. You analyze every possible outcome, trying to make the perfect choice. You go back and forth, second-guessing yourself, fearing that one wrong move will ruin everything. But this level of overanalysis can lead to decision paralysis—where you spend so much time worrying that you never take action at all.

Think about times when you've hesitated to make a decision out of fear. Maybe you stayed in a job that made you miserable because you worried about finding another one. Maybe you delayed taking a risk—applying to a program, starting a business, or moving to a new place—because you couldn't guarantee the outcome. The longer you stayed stuck, the more fearful you became, reinforcing the idea that you weren't ready.

But waiting for the "perfect moment" is an illusion. There will always be unknowns. There will always be risks. And the truth is, not making a decision is still a decision—one that keeps you stuck in the same place.

One way to break free from overthinking is to shift your mindset from perfection to progress. Instead of asking:

- What if I fail? → Ask: What can I learn if this doesn't go as planned?

- What if I make the wrong choice? → Ask: What small step can I take to test the waters?

- What if things don't work out? → Ask: What's the worst that could happen, and can I handle it?

The best way to create a better future is not by worrying about it—it's by taking intentional steps in the present. Every small action builds momentum, and momentum leads to confidence. The sooner you take action, the sooner you gain clarity.

Shifting from Worry to Action

Instead of getting trapped in endless worry, focus on what you *can* do. Here are a few strategies to help you stay grounded:

1. **Limit "What-If" Thinking**

   If you find yourself spiraling into worst-case scenarios, stop and challenge those thoughts. Ask yourself: *Am I predicting disaster without evidence?* Most of the things we worry about never actually happen.

2. **Take One Small Step**

   If a big decision feels overwhelming, break it down into smaller, manageable steps. Taking action, no matter how small, shifts your focus from fear to progress.

3. **Practice Mindfulness**

Mindfulness techniques, like deep breathing and meditation, help train your brain to stay in the present. The more you practice being present, the less power worry has over you.

4. **Trust Yourself**

   You've handled challenges before, and you'll handle them again. Instead of doubting your ability to deal with the future, remind yourself of past obstacles you've overcome.

Worrying about the future won't make it any more predictable or controllable. The only thing you truly have power over is this moment, right now. Instead of wasting energy on what might happen, focus on what you can do today to create the life you want.

Let go of the fear of making the wrong choice. There is no perfect decision—only the decision you make and what you learn from it. Keep moving forward, and trust that clarity will come as you take action.

Nothing kills you faster than your own mind. Be calm—don't stress over things that are out of your control. The more you let go of unnecessary worry, the more space you create for peace, growth, and happiness.

THE POWER OF THE PRESENT MOMENT

Right now, in this very moment, you have the power to make a difference in your life. The present is where real change happens, where growth takes place, and where joy is found.

What Happens When You Stay Present?

- You feel less stressed and more at peace.
- You make better decisions based on what's real, not what-ifs.

- You experience life more fully—conversations are richer, relationships deepen, and small joys become more meaningful.

How to Train Your Mind to Stay Present

Letting go of the past and staying present isn't always easy, but with practice, it becomes second nature. Here are powerful ways to cultivate mindfulness and embrace the now:

1. Practice Mindful Awareness

Mindfulness is the ability to be fully present in the moment without judgment. It's about focusing on what's happening right now instead of getting lost in regrets or worries.

Try this simple exercise:

- Pause and take a deep breath.
- Notice your surroundings—the colors, sounds, and sensations around you.
- Bring your attention to what you're doing. If you're drinking coffee, savor the taste. If you're walking, feel the ground beneath your feet.

The more you practice this, the easier it becomes to stay present.

2. Let Go of Regret with Self-Compassion

If you struggle with letting go of past mistakes, remind yourself: You did the best you could with the knowledge and resources you had at the time.

Self-compassion means treating yourself with the same kindness you would offer a friend. Instead of criticizing yourself for past choices, acknowledge that you're human. Learn from the past, but don't live there.

3. Stop Overthinking and Trust Yourself

Overanalyzing decisions about the future only creates stress. When faced with uncertainty, ask yourself:

- What evidence do I have that this fear will actually come true?
- If I let go of this worry, how would my life change?

Trust that you will handle whatever comes your way, just as you've handled challenges in the past.

4. Release the Need for Perfection

Many people stay stuck in the past or worry about the future because they fear making mistakes. But perfection is an illusion—no one has all the answers, and no one gets everything right.

Instead of striving for perfection, aim for progress. Focus on taking small, consistent steps in the present.

5. Develop a Daily Gratitude Practice

Focusing on what you have right now helps shift your mindset away from what you've lost or what you fear. Try keeping a gratitude journal—every morning, write down three things you're grateful for. Over time, you'll train your brain to focus on the positives in the present.

6. Use Your Senses to Anchor Yourself

Whenever you feel overwhelmed by thoughts of the past or future, use this simple grounding technique:

5-4-3-2-1 Exercise:

- **5 things you see** – Your hands, a tree outside, the book on your desk, a cup of coffee, the sunlight streaming through the window.

- **4 things you touch** – Your shirt, the chair, your phone, the smooth surface of your desk.

- **3 things you hear** – Birds chirping, soft music in the background, your own breath.

- **2 things you smell** – Freshly brewed coffee, the crisp morning air.

- **1 thing you taste** – A hint of mint from your gum.

This brings you back to the present moment, calming your mind instantly.

LIVING IN THE NOW—YOUR KEY TO HAPPINESS AND SUCCESS

Letting go of the past and staying present isn't about ignoring your memories or giving up on your future. It's about shifting your focus to where life is actually happening—*right now.*

- *You can't rewrite the past, but you can learn from it.*

- *You can't control the future, but you can shape it through today's actions.*

- *The present is the only moment that truly belongs to you— make the most of it.*

Every second you spend dwelling on the past or worrying about the future is a second you lose from living today. Choose to let go. Choose to be here, now. Your best life is waiting in the present moment.

Stories of Letting Go and Staying Present

"Do not dwell in the past, do not dream of the future, concentrate the mind on the present moment."

- Buddha

---

1. The Pianist Who Released the Past

Alex had been a pianist since childhood, but one mistake had haunted him for years. During a major competition, his fingers slipped, and that wrong note had echoed in his mind ever since. Every performance afterward was filled with hesitation, as if he were still trying to fix that one moment in time.

One evening, he wandered into an old music shop and saw a battered piano in the corner. He sat down, running his fingers over the keys. Unlike the pristine grand pianos he usually played, this one had chipped edges and slightly uneven tones—imperfect, yet still beautiful.

He closed his eyes and played. The wrong notes blended with the right ones, and for the first time, he didn't stop to correct himself. Music wasn't about perfection; it was about feeling. And in that moment, he finally let go of the performance that had haunted him for so long.

2. The Entrepreneur Who Stopped Fearing the Future

Freya had spent months hesitating. She had a business plan, a savings account, and a dream, but fear gripped her. What if I fail? What if no one buys my pastries?

One rainy afternoon, she found herself watching a street performer juggle flaming torches. He dropped one. The crowd gasped, but he simply picked it up and kept going. No apology, no hesitation.

Freya had been waiting for the perfect moment to start her bakery—no risk, no mistakes. But that street performer didn't wait for perfection; he kept moving, even when things went wrong.

The next morning, she rented a small kitchen and made her first batch of pastries. The fear didn't disappear, but she realized something important: moving forward, even imperfectly, was better than standing still.

3. The Father Who Learned to Be Present

Ethan was always busy. He believed his long hours and packed schedule were necessary for his family's future. But one weekend, while cleaning out old boxes, he found a dusty video camera. Inside was a tape labeled "Lena's 2nd Birthday."

He pressed play, expecting to relive a sweet memory—but as the video rolled, he saw himself in the background, checking his phone, stepping away for calls, never fully there.

His daughter, now ten, walked in as he watched. "Was I funny back then?" she asked.

Ethan nodded, but his chest tightened. He had been so focused on providing a better future that he had missed the present unfolding right in front of him. That night, he put his phone away during dinner. The emails could wait. His daughter's stories about school couldn't.

These stories reveal an important truth: dwelling on the past and fearing the future only take away from the life you could be living right now.

You can't erase mistakes, but you can stop letting them define you. You can't predict the future, but you can take action instead of overthinking. And you can't redo lost time—but you can choose to be fully present in the moments ahead.

CHAPTER 6

FAITH - THE ULTIMATE SOURCE OF GUIDANCE

Faith is more than just a belief—it is a foundation for strength, purpose, and resilience. It is the quiet voice that reassures you in times of uncertainty, the invisible force that pushes you forward when you feel like giving up. Whether you place your faith in God, the universe, or a higher power, this belief gives you the courage to navigate life's challenges with confidence. Faith is not just about religion; it is about trust—trusting in the process, in yourself, and in something greater than your immediate circumstances.

When you cultivate faith, you unlock a sense of peace that cannot be shaken by external events. It keeps you grounded when life feels overwhelming, reminding you that everything happens for a reason and that even in moments of difficulty, there is a lesson to be learned. Faith does not eliminate hardships, but it gives you the strength to overcome them.

FAITH AS A SOURCE OF STRENGTH

Life is unpredictable. No matter how carefully you plan, there will be moments of struggle, loss, and disappointment. Without faith, these moments can feel unbearable—like a storm without shelter. But when you trust that there is a purpose behind every experience, you gain the ability to endure hardships with grace.

Faith is not just about believing that things will get better; it is about knowing that even in the darkest times, you are not alone. It is the anchor that keeps you steady when the waves of life try to pull you under. When you have faith, you develop the resilience to push forward, even when circumstances seem bleak.

Have you ever faced a moment in life when you felt completely lost? Perhaps you were struggling with a difficult decision, facing financial hardship, or dealing with a personal loss. In those moments, it is easy to fall into despair. But faith reminds you that nothing is permanent—situations change, and better days will come.

Faith allows you to focus on the bigger picture instead of being consumed by temporary difficulties. It helps you remain hopeful even when there is no immediate solution in sight. When you truly believe that everything happens for a reason, you start seeing obstacles not as punishments but as opportunities to grow and learn.

Resilience is the ability to bounce back from difficulties. People who lack faith often struggle with resilience because they feel powerless when facing challenges. But faith instills a sense of inner strength—it tells you that you can overcome anything, no matter how difficult it may seem.

When you hold onto faith, you don't just survive challenges; you rise above them. You recognize that hardships are not meant to break you but to shape you into a stronger, wiser person. Every challenge you overcome becomes proof of your ability to persevere, making it easier to face future difficulties with courage and confidence.

Turning Obstacles into Opportunities

Imagine facing a major setback—perhaps a failed business, a lost job, or a broken relationship. Without faith, you may feel lost, questioning your worth and purpose. You may find yourself stuck in self-doubt, believing that this failure defines you. But faith shifts your perspective. Instead of seeing failure as the end, you see it as a redirection toward something greater.

Many of the world's most successful people encountered devastating failures before they found success. What kept them going? Faith. They believed in their purpose, even when circumstances suggested otherwise. When you trust that better things are ahead, you stop fearing failure and start embracing growth.

Every setback carries a lesson. If you lose a job, perhaps it is an opportunity to explore a career that aligns more with your passions. If a relationship ends, maybe it was preparing you for someone better suited for your growth. Faith teaches you to look beyond the pain and see the potential for transformation.

Take, for example, famous figures like Thomas Edison, who failed thousands of times before inventing the light bulb, or Oprah Winfrey, who was fired from her first television job before becoming a global icon. Their faith in themselves and their purpose kept them moving forward despite setbacks. They didn't allow failures to define them; instead, they used them as stepping stones to something greater.

Faith is not just about waiting for things to improve; it encourages action. When you believe that success, healing, or happiness is possible, you take steps toward it. You put in the effort, knowing that the outcome will be worth it.

For example, if you believe you can improve your health, you start making better choices—exercising, eating right, and taking care of yourself. If you believe you can achieve your dreams, you work hard, learn new skills, and keep pushing forward. Faith fuels your determination, making you more proactive in shaping your future.

A strong faith mindset allows you to reframe failure as a learning experience rather than a dead end. Instead of asking, "Why did this happen to me?" you start asking, "What can I learn from this?" This shift in perspective makes all the difference.

Faith gives you the confidence to try again, even after setbacks. It teaches you that rejection and failure are not signals to give up but rather opportunities to grow. When you trust the process, you stop fearing failure and start seeing it as a necessary part of the journey toward success.

Developing an Unshakable Faith

Faith is like a muscle—the more you use it, the stronger it becomes. Here are some ways to cultivate and strengthen your faith:

1. **Stay Positive Even in Difficult Times** – When challenges arise, remind yourself that they are temporary. Focus on solutions instead of problems.

2. **Surround Yourself with Supportive People** – The people you spend time with can influence your mindset. Surround yourself with those who encourage and uplift your faith rather than those who fill you with doubt.

3. **Reflect on Past Successes** – Remind yourself of times when you overcame difficulties. Reflecting on past victories helps reinforce your belief that you can handle whatever comes next.

4. **Practice Gratitude** – Being grateful for what you have shifts your focus from what is missing to what is abundant in your life. Gratitude strengthens faith by helping you see the blessings you already have.

5. **Take Small Steps Forward** – Even when you don't have all the answers, keep moving forward. Take small, consistent steps in the direction of your goals, trusting that each step will bring you closer to where you need to be.

FAITH AND GRATITUDE: A POWERFUL COMBINATION

Faith and gratitude go hand in hand. When you believe that everything is working for your good, you naturally develop a grateful heart. Gratitude shifts your focus from what you lack to what you have, reinforcing your faith in the process of life.

When you start your day with gratitude, you train your mind to see the good in every situation. Even when things don't go as planned, you can find reasons to be thankful. Maybe a delay saved you from an accident, or a rejection redirected you to a better opportunity. Faith allows you to trust that every event—good or bad—serves a greater purpose.

The Science Behind Faith and Gratitude

Research shows that people who practice gratitude experience lower stress, better mental health, and greater overall happiness. Faith works in a similar way—it rewires your brain to focus on hope rather than fear. When you combine faith with gratitude, you create a powerful mindset that attracts positivity into your life.

A grateful heart reinforces your faith, and faith strengthens your gratitude. Together, they create a cycle of positivity, helping you manifest the life you desire.

FAITH IN MANIFESTING YOUR HOPES AND DREAMS

Many people believe that success is purely a result of hard work and talent. While these are important, faith plays an equally crucial role. You must believe in your dreams before they become reality. Without faith, doubt creeps in, leading to hesitation, fear, and ultimately, inaction.

Successful people have one thing in common: they hold an unshakable belief in their vision. Even when faced with doubt, rejection, and obstacles, they trust that what they desire is possible. This untiring faith fuels their persistence, driving them to take action even when success seems distant.

But faith in your dreams is more than just wishful thinking. It is an active trust that what you are working toward will come to fruition. It keeps you going in the face of setbacks, reminding you that failure is not the end—just a lesson along the way.

1. The Power of Faith in Action

Faith is not just about hoping for the best; it is about believing so strongly in your dreams that you take steps toward them with confidence. When you trust in a goal, you naturally align your actions to make it happen. Every small step you take in faith strengthens your belief and moves you closer to your vision.

Consider how many great inventions, businesses, and personal triumphs were born out of faith. People who achieved the impossible did so because they refused to give up, even when others doubted them. Their faith was the driving force behind their determination.

2. The Power of Visualization and Affirmation

Faith is strengthened when you actively see and speak your dreams into existence. Two powerful tools to reinforce faith are visualization and affirmation.

- **Visualization:** Close your eyes and imagine your goals as if they have already been achieved. Picture yourself in your dream job, holding the keys to your new home, or celebrating a personal victory. Feel the emotions of success—joy, gratitude, and excitement. When you do this consistently, your mind begins to accept your vision as reality, making it easier for you to take the necessary steps to bring it to life.

- **Affirmation:** Speak your faith into existence. Words carry power, and what you declare over your life shapes your mindset and actions. Instead of saying, "I hope this happens," say, "I know this will happen." Replace negative self-talk with faith-driven affirmations:

  - "I am capable and prepared for success."

o "The Creator is guiding my path, and I trust His plan."

o "Doors of opportunity are opening for me."

Affirmations rewire your subconscious mind, replacing doubt with belief. When repeated consistently, they shape your reality by reinforcing confidence and attracting opportunities.

3. Overcoming Doubt with Faith

Doubt is a natural part of the journey, but faith allows you to push through uncertainty. Many people give up on their dreams because they don't see immediate results. They assume that delays mean denial, but in reality, waiting is often a test of faith.

Faith is about trusting in *the Universe's timing* rather than your own. Just because something hasn't happened yet doesn't mean it won't. Sometimes, the delay is preparation for something even greater than what you originally envisioned.

When you feel discouraged, remind yourself:

- A higher power has a plan bigger than your fear.

- Obstacles are stepping stones, not roadblocks.

- Faith isn't about seeing results instantly—it's about trusting the process.

Even when your dreams seem far away, trust that they are on their way to you. Having faith in your dreams doesn't mean sitting back and waiting for miracles—it means taking action with confidence. Faith without action is empty, but faith combined with effort leads to transformation.

- **Take the first step:** Don't wait until everything is perfect. Move forward, even if you're uncertain.

- **Keep learning and growing:** Equip yourself with knowledge, skills, and connections that align with your dreams.

- **Surround yourself with faith-driven people:** Avoid negativity and seek out those who encourage and uplift you.

When you combine faith with action, miracles happen. Doors open, opportunities arise, and your path becomes clearer. Even when things don't unfold exactly as you expected, trust that they are happening for you, not to you.

Faith in manifesting your dreams is about believing before you see the results. It is about trusting that a Divine power is working behind the scenes, preparing the right opportunities, people, and timing for your success.

By strengthening your faith, practicing visualization and affirmation, overcoming doubt, and taking intentional action, you set yourself up for extraordinary breakthroughs. Keep believing, keep moving forward, and watch as your dreams unfold in ways beyond what you imagined.

FAITH AS A SOURCE OF PROTECTION AND PEACE

One of the greatest gifts of faith is the sense of peace it provides. Life is filled with uncertainties, but faith reminds you that you are never alone. It reassures you that no matter what happens, you are guided and protected. This deep sense of security is what allows people to move forward with courage, even when the path ahead is unclear.

Many people struggle with anxiety because they try to control everything. But the truth is, control is an illusion. You cannot predict every outcome, nor can you prevent every hardship. Life is unpredictable, and trying to micromanage every detail only creates stress, exhaustion, and frustration.

Faith teaches you to let go. It allows you to surrender your worries, trusting that things will unfold as they should. This does not mean being passive or ignoring your responsibilities—it means doing your best while trusting that everything else will fall into place.

Have you ever noticed how some people remain calm even in the most stressful situations? It's because they have faith. They trust that even when things seem to be going wrong, they are actually falling into place. Faith provides the perspective that challenges are not punishments but opportunities to grow, shift, and evolve.

When you release the need to control every outcome, you open yourself up to greater peace. Instead of being consumed by fear, you can focus on solutions, take things one step at a time, and trust that you will be provided with what you need when the time is right.

Trusting in Divine Timing

A major part of faith is trusting in divine timing. In a world that values instant results, waiting can feel difficult. You may pray for something—a job, a breakthrough, a change—but when it doesn't happen immediately, doubt creeps in.

Faith reminds you that delays are not denials. Just because something hasn't happened yet doesn't mean it won't happen at the right time. Sometimes, what you are waiting for requires preparation. Sometimes, what you want is not what you need. And sometimes, the universe has something even better in store for you than you ever imagined.

When you trust in divine timing, you release frustration. Instead of worrying about when something will happen, you focus on preparing yourself for when it does. You trust that what is meant for you will come—not too soon, not too late, but exactly when it is supposed to.

Patience is one of the greatest tests of faith. But those who trust in universe's timing often find that everything works out far better than they could have planned on their own.

Faith and the Power of Prayer

Prayer is one of the most powerful ways to strengthen faith. It is not just about asking for things—it is about building a connection with the Most High, expressing gratitude, and finding guidance. Prayer shifts your focus from fear to faith, reminding you that you are never alone in your struggles.

Many people find that when they pray consistently, they experience greater peace, clarity, and confidence. Even in the toughest times, prayer provides comfort, reminding you that there is a higher power at work in your life.

Whether it is a simple prayer of thanks, a request for guidance, or a moment of silent reflection, prayer strengthens your faith and brings a sense of protection. It reassures you that you are cared for and that no challenge is too great for The Divine to handle.

Faith is not just for difficult moments—it is a daily practice that transforms the way you live. When you have faith:

- You wake up with gratitude, knowing that each day is a gift.

- You approach challenges with confidence, trusting that you will overcome them.

- You treat others with kindness and compassion, knowing that love is at the heart of faith.

- You move forward without fear, trusting that you are being guided toward your purpose.

Faith is not about having all the answers—it is about trusting even when you don't. It is about knowing that no matter what happens, you are never alone. And when you live with faith, you experience a deep sense of peace, knowing that everything will work out exactly as it should.

CULTIVATING FAITH IN DAILY LIFE

Faith is like a muscle—it grows stronger with practice. If you want to build unwavering faith, you must nurture it daily.

Here are some simple ways to strengthen your faith:

1. **Practice Daily Prayer or Meditation** – Take time each day to connect with your higher power. Whether through prayer, meditation, or reflection, this practice strengthens your faith and brings clarity to your life.

2. **Surround Yourself with Positivity** – Be mindful of the people and influences around you. Surround yourself with those who uplift and encourage your faith.

3. **Keep a Faith Journal** – Write down moments when faith helped you overcome challenges. Reflecting on these experiences reminds you of the power of belief.

4. **Trust the Timing of Your Life** – Not everything happens when you want it to, but that doesn't mean it won't happen. Trust that delays are not denials—they are just a part of the process.

5. **Read Stories of Faith** – Whether from religious texts, biographies, or personal experiences, stories of faith inspire and strengthen your own belief.

Faith is not just something you have—it is something you cultivate, something you live by every day.

Faith is the foundation upon which lasting success and fulfillment are built. It gives you the strength to overcome obstacles, the hope to pursue your dreams, and the peace to trust the journey. When you cultivate faith, you open yourself to a life of purpose, joy, and resilience.

No matter where you are in life, know that faith is always available to you. It is a choice you make every day—to trust in something greater than yourself, to believe in your path, and to move forward with confidence.

When you embrace faith, you transform fear into courage, doubt into determination, and challenges into opportunities. And most importantly, you discover that everything you need has been within you all along.

STORIES OF FAITH AND STRENGTH

---

*"Faith and fear both demand you believe in
something you cannot see. You choose."*

- Bob Proctor

---

1. The Traveler's Trust – Believing in the Journey

Omar had always been a careful planner, mapping out every step
of his life. But when a sudden job loss forced him to rethink
everything, he felt completely lost. He had always believed that hard
work guaranteed success, but now he questioned everything.

With no clear direction, he packed a small bag and decided to take
a journey through the countryside—a trip with no set destination, only
a desire to clear his mind. Along the way, he met strangers who shared
kindness, unexpected opportunities that seemed to appear at the right
moment, and lessons that changed his outlook on life.

One evening, as he sat by a quiet river, an elderly man he had met
on the road said, *"Sometimes, when the road is unclear, you just have
to take the next step in faith. The path will reveal itself."*

Omar realized that faith wasn't about knowing every answer in
advance—it was about trusting that, even in uncertainty, life had a
way of unfolding just as it should.

2. The Lost Son – Finding Redemption

David had strayed far from the path he was raised on. He had
chased wealth, status, and the pleasures of the world, only to find
himself empty and alone. His reckless decisions had cost him his
friendships, his job, and his peace of mind.

One night, wandering aimlessly through the streets, he passed by
a small community center. The sound of laughter and music drifted

from inside. Something stirred in him—a memory of a time when he had felt connected, when life had meaning beyond personal success.

For the first time in years, he stopped, took a deep breath, and stepped inside. He was welcomed with warmth, no questions asked. That night, he felt a peace he hadn't known in years. He started reconnecting with his family, rebuilding his life, and making amends.

He realized that no matter how far he had fallen, grace and second chances were always within reach.

3. The Mother's Hope – Trusting in Life's Timing

Miriam was a single mother struggling to provide for her two young children. With no steady job and bills piling up, she found herself at the edge of despair. She had no idea how she would put food on the table the next day.

As she sat at the kitchen table, she took a deep breath and reminded herself of the times she had faced hardship before—and how, somehow, she had always found a way through.

The next morning, there was a knock on her door. A woman from the neighborhood stood there with bags of groceries. "I don't know why," she said, "but I felt like I needed to bring this to you today."

Tears filled Miriam's eyes. At that moment, she realized that faith wasn't about seeing a solution—it was about trusting that one would come.

4. The Doctor's Hands – Trusting in Something Greater

Dr. Elijah Carter had spent years in medical school, training to save lives. But on one particular evening, standing in the operating room, he faced a situation that no textbook could prepare him for. A young girl had been rushed in after a severe accident, and her chances of survival were slim.

As the machines beeped around him and the nurses stood ready, Elijah's hands trembled. He had done everything medically possible, but there was no certainty she would pull through.

In that moment of helplessness, he closed his eyes and whispered to himself, *"Let me do what I can, and let the rest be guided by something greater."*

A sense of calm washed over him. He took a deep breath, steadied his hands, and proceeded with the surgery. Hours later, as dawn broke, the young girl stabilized. It was nothing short of a miracle.

Later, her mother tearfully thanked him, but Elijah knew the truth. "I did what I could," he said, "but sometimes, we're just instruments in something greater than ourselves."

These stories remind us that faith isn't about having all the answers—it's about trusting in the journey, even when we can't see the way forward. Whether you're facing struggles, doubts, or uncertainty, faith assures you that you're never alone.

The path ahead may be unclear, but trust that it is unfolding exactly as it should. If you hold on to faith—whatever that means to you—life will guide you, provide for you, and lead you toward something greater than you ever imagined.

CHAPTER 7

THE POWER OF HUMILITY AND AUTHENTICITY

Humility is often misunderstood. Many people associate it with weakness or passivity, but in reality, humility is a strength. It is the foundation of true leadership, meaningful relationships, and lasting success. When you embrace humility, you open yourself up to learning, growth, and deeper connections with those around you.

In both professional and personal life, humility allows you to step back, acknowledge that you don't have all the answers, and invite others to contribute. It fosters trust, encourages collaboration, and builds a culture where people feel valued and respected. If you want to be a strong leader, a successful professional, or simply a better human being, humility must be at the core of your approach.

THE TRUE MEANING OF HUMILITY

Humility does not mean thinking less of yourself—it means thinking of yourself less. It's not about downplaying your achievements or pretending to be less capable than you are. Instead, it's about recognizing that your strengths and talents are valuable, but they do not make you superior to others.

A humble person acknowledges their successes while also understanding that no one achieves greatness alone. Whether you're leading a company, working as part of a team, or striving for personal goals, humility allows you to appreciate the contributions of others and recognize that learning is a lifelong process.

HUMILITY IN LEADERSHIP: THE KEY TO TRUST AND INFLUENCE

If you're in a leadership role—whether you're managing a team, running a business, or mentoring others—your humility (or lack of it) will define the culture you create. Humble leaders are approachable, open to feedback, and willing to admit when they're wrong. They don't let their egos get in the way of making the best decisions.

Think about the best leaders you've encountered. Were they the ones who always had to be right? The ones who refused to listen to others? Or were they the ones who took the time to understand different perspectives, encouraged collaboration, and admitted when they made mistakes?

Humility in leadership builds trust. When people see that you value their input, they feel empowered to share their ideas. They are more likely to be honest about challenges and contribute to meaningful solutions. On the other hand, when a leader lacks humility—when they act as though they are the smartest person in the room—people hesitate to speak up. Innovation stalls, morale drops, and trust erodes.

How to Cultivate Humility as a Leader

1. **Listen More Than You Speak** – The best leaders listen attentively. When someone speaks, give them your full attention. Avoid interrupting or thinking about your response while they are talking.

2. **Admit When You're Wrong** – No one is right all the time. When you make a mistake, own it. Apologize if necessary, and focus on how you can improve.

3. **Give Credit to Others** – A humble leader acknowledges the contributions of their team. Instead of taking credit for success, recognize and celebrate the people who made it happen.

4. **Ask for Feedback** – Regularly seek feedback from those you lead. Ask them what you can do better and be willing to act on their suggestions.

5. **Stay Teachable** – No matter how experienced or successful you are, there is always more to learn. Stay curious and open to new ideas.

THE ROLE OF HUMILITY IN PERSONAL GROWTH

Beyond leadership, humility is essential for personal growth. It allows you to see your own shortcomings without shame and gives you the courage to improve. If you believe you already know everything, you close yourself off from learning. But when you remain humble, you acknowledge that there is always room to grow.

Humility helps you become more self-aware. It enables you to recognize areas where you can improve without feeling threatened or defensive. This kind of self-awareness is a key driver of success because it allows you to continuously refine your skills, habits, and mindset.

People who lack humility often struggle with personal growth because they resist constructive criticism. They may view feedback as a personal attack rather than an opportunity for improvement. However, those who embrace humility understand that growth comes from acknowledging weaknesses and actively working to overcome them. When you approach life with humility, you become more receptive to learning experiences, more willing to step out of your comfort zone, and more resilient in the face of challenges.

Embracing Mistakes as Learning Opportunities

Everyone makes mistakes. But the way you respond to those mistakes determines whether they become roadblocks or stepping stones. If you let pride take over, you may try to justify your errors or shift blame to others. This prevents growth. But when you approach mistakes with humility, you can reflect on what went wrong, take responsibility, and make better choices moving forward.

Rather than fearing failure, humility allows you to reframe it as part of the learning process. When you acknowledge mistakes without letting them define you, you build resilience. You begin to see setbacks as temporary obstacles rather than permanent defeats.

Think of some of the most successful people in the world—entrepreneurs, artists, athletes. Most of them didn't achieve greatness on their first attempt. They failed, they learned, and they kept going. Humility is what allowed them to accept failure as part of the journey rather than as a reason to quit.

Consider Thomas Edison, who famously tested thousands of materials before successfully inventing the light bulb. He viewed each failed attempt as a step closer to success rather than as a reason to stop trying. When asked about his many failures, he simply said, "I have not failed. I've just found 10,000 ways that won't work." This mindset—rooted in humility—allowed him to persist where others might have given up.

To apply this in your own life, start seeing mistakes as opportunities to grow. Ask yourself:

- What can I learn from this experience?

- How can I improve next time?

- What adjustments can I make to achieve a better outcome?

When you embrace humility, you develop the ability to turn failures into stepping stones toward success.

The Power of Vulnerability

Humility also allows you to embrace vulnerability. Many people associate vulnerability with weakness, but it is actually a sign of strength. When you are willing to be open and honest—about your struggles, your fears, and your uncertainties—you create space for deeper connections.

Vulnerability does not mean oversharing or exposing your weaknesses without purpose. It means having the courage to be authentic, to admit when you need help, and to acknowledge that you don't have all the answers. When you do this, you encourage others to do the same, fostering an environment of trust and mutual support.

People are drawn to authenticity. When you drop the need to appear perfect and instead show up as your true self, others feel safe doing the same. This strengthens relationships, whether in the workplace, at home, or within your community.

In professional settings, leaders who embrace vulnerability can inspire their teams in profound ways. When a leader admits they don't have all the answers but are willing to learn, it empowers others to contribute their own insights. It creates an atmosphere where people feel valued and heard. On the other hand, when leaders refuse to show vulnerability, employees may feel hesitant to speak up, fearing judgment or criticism.

In personal relationships, vulnerability deepens connections. It allows for honest communication, fosters empathy, and helps build meaningful bonds. When you are willing to share your challenges, others feel comfortable sharing theirs as well, leading to mutual support and understanding.

How to Cultivate Humility and Embrace Vulnerability

1. **Practice Self-Reflection** – Regularly take time to evaluate your actions, decisions, and attitudes. Ask yourself where you can improve and what lessons you can take from past experiences.

2. **Seek Feedback** – Be open to constructive criticism. Instead of reacting defensively, listen with the intention to learn and grow.

3. **Recognize That You Don't Have All the Answers** – Accepting that you are not always right creates opportunities for learning and growth. Be open to different perspectives and ideas.

4. **Acknowledge the Contributions of Others** – Whether in your personal or professional life, express gratitude and recognize the efforts of those around you.

5. **Share Your Struggles** – If you are comfortable, open up about challenges you have faced. Doing so creates deeper connections and encourages others to do the same.

6. **Embrace Discomfort** – Growth often comes from stepping outside of your comfort zone. Be willing to try new things, take risks, and face challenges with an open mind.

By incorporating humility and vulnerability into your daily life, you set yourself up for continuous growth, stronger relationships, and greater success. These qualities will not only make you a better leader but also a more compassionate and understanding person.

HUMILITY AND AUTHENTICITY IN THE WORKPLACE

A workplace that values humility and authenticity is one where people feel respected, appreciated, and heard. When employees know that their leaders and colleagues are open to feedback, willing to learn, and focused on collective success rather than personal gain, they are more engaged and motivated.

Humility fosters an environment where everyone feels empowered to contribute, regardless of their position or experience level. When leaders demonstrate humility, they encourage collaboration rather than competition, ensuring that team members work together toward common goals. This kind of workplace culture creates a sense of belonging and psychological safety, where employees feel comfortable sharing their ideas and concerns without fear of judgment.

THE BENEFITS OF A HUMBLE AND AUTHENTIC WORKPLACE CULTURE

A culture of humility leads to:

1. **Better teamwork** – Employees feel comfortable sharing ideas and collaborating without fear of being dismissed or criticized. This openness leads to stronger problem-solving and innovation.

2. **Higher job satisfaction** – People enjoy working in an environment where they feel valued and where their contributions are recognized, leading to higher engagement and morale.

3. **Stronger innovation** – When employees are not afraid of being wrong, they take more creative risks, leading to groundbreaking ideas and improvements. A humble workplace encourages experimentation and learning from mistakes.

4. **Healthier conflict resolution** – Humility allows people to approach disagreements with a focus on understanding rather than defending their ego. This reduces workplace tension and encourages productive conversations.

5. **Increased trust and loyalty** – Employees are more likely to trust leaders who admit their mistakes, acknowledge their limitations, and prioritize the well-being of the team. This trust translates into long-term loyalty and commitment.

HOW LEADERS CAN FOSTER HUMILITY AND AUTHENTICITY

Leaders play a crucial role in shaping workplace culture. When they model humility, it sets the tone for the entire organization. Here are some ways leaders can cultivate humility and authenticity:

1. **Encourage Open Communication** – Create an environment where employees feel safe to express their thoughts, ask questions, and share concerns. Actively listen and show genuine interest in their perspectives.

2. **Admit Mistakes and Learn from Them** – A leader who acknowledges their own mistakes demonstrates strength, not weakness. When you take responsibility for errors and show a willingness to learn, employees are more likely to do the same.

3. **Give Credit Where It's Due** – Recognize and celebrate the contributions of team members. Avoid taking sole credit for successes and instead highlight the efforts of those who made achievements possible.

4. **Seek Feedback from Employees** – Regularly ask for input on how you can improve as a leader. This not only helps you grow but also reinforces a culture of continuous learning and development.

5. **Be Approachable and Relatable** – Leaders who are humble and authentic connect more easily with their teams. Share your challenges and lessons learned to inspire and guide others.

PRACTICAL WAYS TO PRACTICE HUMILITY DAILY

Humility isn't just a trait for leaders; it's something everyone can cultivate in their daily work and interactions. Here are some practical ways to integrate humility into your routine:

1. Express Gratitude

Regularly acknowledge the people who contribute to your success. This can be as simple as thanking a colleague for their support, recognizing a mentor for their guidance, or appreciating an employee for their hard work. Gratitude fosters a positive work environment and strengthens relationships.

2. Be Open to Different Perspectives

Instead of assuming you know best, actively seek out and consider viewpoints that challenge your own. Engage in discussions with colleagues from different backgrounds and experiences. Being receptive to new ideas broadens your understanding and enhances problem-solving abilities.

3. Serve Others Without Expecting Anything in Return

True humility is demonstrated through service. Look for opportunities to help those around you—whether by mentoring a junior colleague, assisting a teammate with a project, or simply being a supportive presence. Small acts of kindness contribute to a more collaborative and respectful workplace.

4. Acknowledge Your Limitations

It's okay not to have all the answers. Admitting this doesn't make you less competent; rather, it makes you more credible and relatable. Recognizing your limitations allows you to seek input from others, fostering teamwork and collective growth.

5. Let Go of the Need for Recognition

Do good work because it matters, not because you want applause. True humility means being content even when no one is watching. When you focus on contributing value rather than seeking validation, you build a reputation for integrity and reliability.

6. Approach Feedback with a Growth Mindset

Instead of reacting defensively to constructive criticism, view it as an opportunity for improvement. Ask clarifying questions, reflect on the feedback, and implement changes where necessary. A humble mindset transforms feedback into a tool for personal and professional development.

7. Celebrate the Success of Others

A humble person does not feel threatened by the success of their colleagues. Instead of competing, genuinely celebrate their achievements. This not only strengthens workplace relationships but also fosters an environment of mutual respect and encouragement.

THE LONG-TERM IMPACT OF HUMILITY IN THE WORKPLACE

Humility is not just a personal virtue; it has a lasting impact on workplace culture and overall organizational success. Companies that prioritize humility and authenticity tend to have:

- **Lower employee turnover** – People are more likely to stay in an environment where they feel valued and respected.

- **Higher levels of collaboration** – Teams function more effectively when ego does not get in the way of cooperation.

- **Stronger leadership development** – A culture that embraces humility encourages continuous learning and self-improvement.

- **Better decision-making** – Leaders who are open to input and willing to acknowledge their limitations make more informed and balanced decisions.

When you practice humility, you build stronger relationships, gain deeper wisdom, and become a more effective leader. Humility helps you navigate challenges with grace and resilience because you are not driven by ego but by a genuine desire to learn, contribute, and grow.

In the end, humility leads to a more fulfilling life. It allows you to focus on what truly matters—authentic connections, continuous learning, and meaningful contributions. By embracing humility, you not only improve yourself but also create a positive impact on those around you.

Success is not measured by how much power or recognition you gain, but by the positive influence you have on others. Humility is not a weakness—it is the foundation of true strength. When you lead with humility and authenticity, you inspire those around you and build a legacy that lasts.

THE BALANCE OF HUMILITY AND AUTHENTICITY

Authenticity without humility is incomplete. While being true to yourself is important, honesty without humility can sometimes be harsh or even harmful. True authenticity isn't just about saying what's on your mind—it's about expressing yourself in a way that respects and uplifts others.

Humility comes from within; it's the quiet confidence of knowing your worth without needing to prove it at the expense of others. Arrogance, on the other hand, disguises itself as authenticity but lacks the grace that makes honesty meaningful. A person who is brutally honest without humility may believe they are being real, but in truth, they are being reckless.

For authenticity to have true value, it must be grounded in humility. When you are humble, you are not only true to yourself but also considerate of others. You recognize that your perspective is not the only one and that honesty should be delivered with kindness.

Humility and authenticity must always coexist - because when you are humble, you are at your most authentic.

STORIES OF HUMILITY AND AUTHENTICITY

"True humility is not thinking less of yourself; it is thinking of yourself less."

- C.S. Lewis

---

1. The Humble CEO – Leading by Example

Mark Reynolds was the CEO of a thriving tech company. Unlike many executives who preferred the spotlight, Mark made it a point to visit his employees on the ground floor, listening to their concerns and learning about their challenges firsthand. He never saw himself as above anyone—whether it was a junior intern or a longtime manager.

One day, during a major product launch, a sudden technical failure threatened to derail months of hard work. Instead of placing blame, Mark rolled up his sleeves and worked alongside his engineers late into the night. His humility set the tone for the entire company. Employees felt valued, knowing their leader was not just a figurehead but a part of the team.

When asked about his leadership style, Mark simply said, "A leader's job is not to be served but to serve. The best ideas don't always come from the top—they come from those who do the work every day."

Because of his humility, Mark's company flourished, not just in profits but in culture. His employees were loyal, innovative, and willing to go the extra mile because they knew their contributions truly mattered.

2. The Apprentice Carpenter – Learning Through Humility

Diego was eager to become a master carpenter. Fresh out of trade school, he joined an experienced woodworking shop, confident in his abilities. However, whenever his mentor, Mr. Carter, corrected his technique, Diego found himself bristling with frustration.

One day, after botching an important cabinet installation, Diego sighed in frustration. Instead of scolding him, Mr. Carter handed him a chisel and said, "The wood doesn't care how much you know—it only responds to patience and skill. Mastery comes from admitting what you don't know and learning from those who do."

Diego realized his pride had been holding him back. From that moment on, he asked more questions, paid closer attention, and accepted guidance with an open mind. Over the years, he became a skilled carpenter, respected not just for his craftsmanship but for his willingness to learn.

3. The Teacher Who Learned – A Lesson in Listening

Ms. Simmons had been a teacher for over 30 years, and she prided herself on her expertise. She had taught thousands of students and thought she had seen it all. But when a new student, Elena, struggled in her class despite being intelligent, Ms. Simmons assumed the girl simply wasn't trying hard enough.

One day, Elena timidly asked if she could explain something her way. At first, Ms. Simmons dismissed the idea. But then she remembered something she always told her students: *"Learning is a two-way street."* Taking her own advice, she sat down and listened.

Elena's explanation was insightful, offering a fresh perspective on the subject. Ms. Simmons realized she had been too rigid in her teaching style. From then on, she made an effort to hear her students' perspectives, becoming an even better educator in the process.

She often told her fellow teachers, *"Humility isn't about knowing everything—it's about knowing you always have more to learn."*

4. The Honest Athlete – Winning with Integrity

Mia was a star sprinter, known for her speed and determination. During the final race of her high school career, she was neck and neck with her biggest rival. As they approached the finish line, her competitor stumbled slightly, giving Mia the advantage.

She crossed the finish line first, securing the gold medal. But instead of celebrating, she approached the judges and said, "She tripped because of a loose track piece. It wasn't a fair race." The officials reviewed the footage and agreed to a rematch.

Many questioned her decision—after all, she had won fair and square, right? But Mia knew that true success wasn't just about winning—it was about integrity. In the rematch, she ran her heart out and won again, this time with no doubts.

When asked why she had spoken up, she simply said, "Winning means nothing if you don't earn it the right way."

These stories show that humility is not about weakness—it is about strength, authenticity, and the willingness to grow. Whether you are a leader, a learner, a teacher, or an athlete, humility shapes the way you navigate challenges and build relationships.

A life lived with humility leads to deeper connections, greater success, and a legacy that goes beyond personal achievements. When you embrace humility, you open the door to endless learning, meaningful impact, and true fulfillment.

CHAPTER 8

BUILDING A LEGACY OF SUCCESS AND FULFILLMENT

Success is often measured by milestones—career achievements, financial stability, recognition. But a true legacy goes beyond personal accomplishments. It is the impact you leave on others, the values you instill, and the difference you make in the world.

Building a meaningful legacy requires more than just ambition; it demands intentional living. It means making choices that align with your core values, cultivating relationships that matter, and leaving behind something that will endure long after you're gone.

DEFINING SUCCESS ON YOUR TERMS

Many people chase success without ever defining what it means to them. Society often presents a narrow view of success—titles, wealth, status—but these things alone do not guarantee fulfillment. True success is deeply personal. It is about living in alignment with your values and knowing that your contributions matter.

To build a legacy that lasts, ask yourself:

- What do I want to be remembered for?

- What values guide my decisions?

- How am I impacting the people around me?

- Am I building something that will outlive my time in this role, business, or life?

When you define success on your own terms, you take control of your journey. You shift from chasing external validation to creating a life that is rich in meaning and purpose.

THE POWER OF VALUES IN LEGACY-BUILDING

Your values are the foundation of your legacy. They shape the way you lead, work, and connect with others. When your actions align with your values, you create a legacy that is authentic and enduring.

Values are the invisible threads that hold a legacy together. While achievements and accolades may fade over time, the principles you live by leave a lasting imprint. When you uphold your values consistently, they become a guiding light—not just for yourself but for those who follow in your footsteps.

How Values Shape Your Legacy

Consider individuals who are widely admired—not just for their achievements, but for their integrity, kindness, and vision. What makes their legacies stand the test of time? It is their unwavering commitment to their principles.

- **Integrity builds trust.** A person who consistently acts with honesty and fairness earns the respect of those around them. When people remember you as someone who kept their word, upheld ethical standards, and led with sincerity, your legacy gains strength.

- **Kindness leaves a lasting impact.** A simple act of kindness can change someone's life. Whether in business, leadership, or personal relationships, people remember those who treated them with respect and compassion.

- **Resilience sets an example for future generations.** Life is full of challenges, but how you respond to setbacks defines your legacy. When you persevere with courage and determination, you show others that success is not about avoiding failure but learning from it.

- **Service creates a ripple effect.** Many of history's most admired figures are those who dedicated themselves to helping others. Whether through philanthropy, mentorship, or everyday generosity, giving back ensures that your influence extends far beyond your lifetime.

BUILDING A VALUES-BASED LEGACY

To ensure your legacy reflects your values, you must be intentional about how you live each day. Small, consistent actions often have a greater impact than a single grand gesture.

1. Identify Your Core Beliefs

What truly matters to you? Your legacy will be shaped by the principles you prioritize. Take time to reflect on the values that guide your decisions. Ask yourself:

- What are the non-negotiable standards I live by?
- How do I want to be remembered by my family, colleagues, and community?
- What causes or beliefs do I want to champion?

Your values should be deeply personal and not dictated by societal pressures. True legacy-building begins with a clear understanding of who you are and what you stand for.

2. Live by Your Values Every Day

A legacy is built in the small, everyday moments, not just in grand achievements. Integrity, kindness, and service must be evident in your daily actions.

- If honesty is a core value, practice transparency in your business and personal relationships.

- If generosity is important to you, look for opportunities to give—whether time, knowledge, or resources.

- If resilience defines you, face challenges head-on and inspire others by how you handle adversity.

People may not always remember your exact words, but they will remember how you made them feel and the example you set.

3. Pass Your Values On

A meaningful legacy is not just about personal success—it is about inspiring and uplifting others. Your values should not end with you; they should continue through the people you influence.

- **Mentorship:** Teach and guide others, whether in your profession, community, or family. Share your experiences and lessons learned.

- **Leadership by example:** People are more likely to adopt values when they see them in action. Be the person who demonstrates the principles you advocate for.

- **Storytelling:** Share stories of your challenges, successes, and lessons. Stories are powerful tools that help pass on values in a relatable and memorable way.

A strong legacy isn't just about what you accomplish; it's about how you inspire others to uphold those same values long after you're gone.

Leaving a Legacy That Matters

Your legacy is not defined by your job title, the size of your bank account, or the awards you receive. It is defined by the lives you touch and the values you instill in others.

Ask yourself:

- Am I living in a way that reflects my deepest beliefs?

- Am I treating people with the respect and kindness I want to be remembered for?

- Am I making a difference in the world, even in small ways?

Your legacy is not something you create at the end of your life—it is something you build every day through your choices, actions, and the example you set. When your life is guided by strong values, your impact will be felt for generations to come.

SUCCESS AND FULFILLMENT GO HAND IN HAND

Success without fulfillment is empty. Many people achieve their goals only to find themselves feeling unfulfilled, as though something is missing. The key to building a legacy of true success is ensuring that your accomplishments align with your sense of purpose and well-being.

To create both success and fulfillment:

- **Pursue work that is meaningful** – Whether in your career, business, or community, choose paths that bring you a sense of purpose.

- **Cultivate deep relationships** – Success means little if you have no one to share it with. Build strong connections with family, friends, and colleagues.

- **Make a difference** – Look beyond personal gain and focus on how you can contribute to others. Whether through mentorship, philanthropy, or service, leaving an impact on others is the ultimate fulfillment.

When you focus on both achievement and meaning, your success becomes more than just personal—it becomes a gift to the world.

THE ROLE OF HAPPINESS AND SIMPLICITY IN LASTING IMPACT

A legacy isn't just about big accomplishments; it's about the way you live each day. Happiness and simplicity play a crucial role in building a life that others admire and wish to emulate.

Many people believe that success requires constant sacrifice, stress, and overwork. But in reality, the most impactful individuals are those who find joy in their journey and approach life with clarity and balance.

- **Happiness is contagious** – When you find joy in your work and relationships, you inspire others to do the same.

- **Simplicity creates clarity** – A cluttered life can lead to a cluttered mind. Simplify where you can, focusing on what truly matters.

- **Contentment is a form of success** – If you live with gratitude and appreciation for the present moment, you've already achieved something many never do.

Your legacy is shaped not just by what you achieve, but by how you live. A life of joy and purpose leaves a lasting impression.

HEALTH AND WELL-BEING: THE FOUNDATION OF A STRONG LEGACY

Many people work tirelessly to build success but neglect their well-being in the process. A lasting legacy requires longevity—both in terms of physical health and emotional resilience.

To ensure you have the energy and clarity to make a lasting impact:

- **Prioritize self-care** – You can't pour from an empty cup. Take care of your body, mind, and spirit.

- **Balance ambition with rest** – Hard work is important, but burnout prevents long-term impact. Learn when to pause and recharge.

- **Lead by example** – If you encourage others to prioritize well-being while neglecting your own, your message loses its power. Live the principles you want others to follow.

A legacy is not built in a day, but over a lifetime. Taking care of yourself ensures you have the time and energy to leave a meaningful mark.

FAITH AND PURPOSE: THE DEEPER MEANING BEHIND SUCCESS

For many, faith—whether spiritual or simply a strong belief in purpose—plays a role in defining their legacy. Having a sense of purpose gives direction to your work and relationships.

Faith, in any form, can be a guiding force that keeps you grounded. It reminds you that your impact goes beyond the material world and that your life has significance beyond personal achievements.

To cultivate a purpose-driven legacy:

- **Stay connected to what inspires you** – Whether it's faith, a cause, or a personal mission, let it guide your decisions.

- **Trust the process** – Success is not always immediate, but patience and faith in your path can keep you moving forward.

- **Remember that impact outlasts recognition** – True legacy isn't about how many people know your name—it's about how many lives you touch.

When your success is rooted in purpose, it carries weight far beyond financial gain or professional status.

Living with Legacy in Mind

Your legacy isn't something you build at the end of your life—it's something you create every day. Each decision you make, each relationship you nurture, each value you uphold contributes to the mark you leave on the world.

To ensure your legacy is one of success and fulfillment:

- **Define what success means to you** – Don't let society dictate your path.

- **Live by your values** – Align your actions with what truly matters.

- **Balance achievement with happiness** – Success should feel fulfilling, not exhausting.

- **Prioritize relationships and well-being** – The people you impact will carry your legacy forward.

- **Trust in your purpose** – Have faith that your contributions matter, even when results aren't immediate.

A life well-lived is the greatest legacy of all. When you lead with intention, prioritize meaning over recognition, and stay true to your values, you leave behind something that endures—a legacy of success, fulfillment, and lasting impact.

TIMELESS LESSONS FOR A LIFE WELL-LIVED

1. Do Not Conform—Transform Others

Never change who you are just to fit into the wrong crowd. The world may pressure you to conform, but true strength lies in standing firm in your values. Instead of being influenced by negativity, be the one who leads others toward the right path.

2. Discipline: The Bridge to Success

Many people look back with regret, wondering what they could have achieved if they had been more disciplined. Success does not happen by chance—it is built through consistent effort, self-control, and perseverance. Stay disciplined, and you will create a life free from regret.

3. Master Your Temper, Protect Your Peace

Uncontrolled anger can destroy relationships, cause unnecessary stress, and lead to regret. Before you react in frustration, take a deep breath and choose wisdom over impulse. Self-control is not weakness—it is a sign of true strength.

4. The Power of Forgiveness

Holding onto resentment is like carrying a heavy burden that weighs you down. Forgiveness is not about justifying another's actions; it is about freeing yourself. Let go of past hurts and embrace peace—you deserve it.

5. Prayer: A Conversation with the Divine

Prayer is more than a ritual; it is a direct connection with God, the universe, or whatever higher power you believe in. It provides guidance, clarity, and inner strength. Never underestimate the power of faith and reflection in shaping your journey.

6. Beware of Manipulation

Some people manipulate and exploit others for their own gain. Narcissistic personalities exist in families, workplaces, and communities, often leaving behind hurt and destruction. Recognize the signs, set boundaries, and, if possible, help them find peace— because a better world starts with individuals who choose healing over harm.

7. Your Words Are More Powerful Than You Realize

The tongue is more dangerous than dynamite. Words can heal or destroy, uplift or tear down. Be mindful of what you say, both to yourself and others. Use your voice to bring light into the world.

8. Love Is the Greatest Legacy

We enter this world with nothing and leave with nothing. What remains is not our wealth or possessions but the love we have shared and the kindness we have shown. Let love be the legacy you leave behind.

These are not just lessons; they are guiding principles for a life of meaning, fulfillment, and joy. Live with purpose, love deeply, and walk your path with integrity.

A NOTE FROM THE AUTHOR

A piece of my heart, specially curated for my readers.

Dear Reader,

As you turn the final pages of this book, I want to leave you with a message from my heart to yours. This is more than just words on a page—it is a reflection of the values, lessons, and wisdom that have shaped my life. It is my hope that they will inspire and guide you in your own journey.

At the core of a meaningful life lies love, respect, and trust. These are the pillars that hold families together, the foundation upon which true happiness is built. In a world that often encourages self-interest, I have come to learn that fulfillment is not found in wealth or recognition, but in the love we give, the lives we touch, and the legacy we leave behind.

Parents have the greatest responsibility of all—to nurture, guide, and uplift their children so they may walk confidently into the world. Love and leadership in the home shape not only the future of our children but of generations to come. A father's love for a mother teaches a daughter what to seek in a partner; a mother's respect for a father shows a son how to love with honor. Parenting is not just about providing; it is about preparing—equipping our children with the strength to overcome obstacles and the wisdom to lead with integrity.

Nature itself offers powerful lessons. The eagle teaches its young to fly, but it does not abandon them before they are ready. The lion protects its cubs fiercely until they can stand on their own. So must we, as parents, mentors, and leaders, guide those entrusted to us with both love and discipline. When we pour our hearts into raising strong individuals, we do more than shape a family—we shape the world.

And what of our own lives? What of the journey we walk each day? I look at myself in the mirror, at 63 years young, and I see not just a body but a spirit still filled with energy, purpose, and gratitude. The human body is a masterpiece, a finely tuned machine designed to last. If we care for it—through nourishment, movement, and a positive mindset—it will carry us further than we ever imagined. Aging is not the passing of years; it is the neglect of the soul and body. When we fuel both with love and care, we thrive.

I have shared these lessons with you not just as words, but as a personal testimony. I stand before you not as someone who has had everything handed to him, but as someone who has faced challenges and found strength in faith, love, and perseverance. If an orphan boy like me can embrace this path, so can you. Keep your spirit childlike—curious, open, and filled with faith. Seek guidance from a higher power, collaborate with those around you, and move forward with love. Do this, and you will not only find joy but also uncover your true purpose in life.

There will come a day when each of us must leave this world. We will take nothing with us—no riches, no titles, no possessions. But what we leave behind is what truly matters. Our legacy is not measured by what we accumulate, but by the love we give, the kindness we show, and the lives we change.

So I ask you now, as you close this book—what will your legacy be? If you lead with love, serve with humility, and live with purpose, I promise you, you will never look back with regret. You will look back and see a life well lived—a legacy that endures.

With all my heart, *Fidel*

www.ingramcontent.com/pod-product-compliance
Lightning Source LLC
LaVergne TN
LVHW011754070326
832904LV00034B/294